SOPHISTICATED
SURFACES

ROCKPORT

First published in the United States of America by:
Rockport Publishers, Inc.
33 Commercial Street
Gloucester, Massachusetts 01930-5089
Telephone: (978) 282-9590
Fax: (978) 283-2742
www.rockpub.com

ISBN 1-56496-873-1

10 9 8 7 6 5 4 3 2

Book Design: Wren Design, Philadelphia, PA
Cover Design: Fahrenheit Design, Lincoln, MA

Front Cover Images (clockwise from top): Martin Alan Hirsch, photo by
Randy McCaffery; Jeff Entner, photo by Peter Simon Photography; Suzanne
Mastroluca, photo by John Vaughan, courtesy of the artist; Leslie Ann
Powers, photo by Tom Hopkins; Suzanne Mastroluca, photo by John
Vaughan, courtesy of the artist
Back Cover Images (clockwise from top): Warnock Studios; Jeff Entner,
photo by Peter Simon; Patti Bruce; Julie Sims Messenger, photo by Kit Pyne
Photography

Printed in China.

SOPHISTICATED SURFACES

GLOUCESTER MASSACHUSETTS

ROCKPORT PUBLISHERS

Ideas and Inspirations from
Eighteen Professional Surface Painters

Karen Aude

Dedication and Acknowledgments

Dedicated to my friends with love,

and with my thanks for their steadfast support and friendship

I would also like to thank my editor Jeanine Caunt for her guidance,

and copyeditor Karyn Bober Kuhn for a super job.

Contents

8 **Introduction**

10 Faux and Fantasy Finishes

12 **Bopas**

20 **Charlene Ayuso Cooper**
FAUXFinish Studio, Inc.

28 **Jeff Entner**

36 **Joe Fenzl**
Decorative Arts of Los Angeles

44 **Martin Alan Hirsch**
Decorative Finishes Studio

52 Painted Surfaces

54 **Dale Wade and Helen Doane**

62 **Kathy McDonald**

70 **John Parsons**

78 **Michael Tyson Murphy**

84 **Suzanne Mastroluca**
Impressions In Paint

92 **Peter Brian Daly**
Artscope Enterprizes

98 **Robert A. Fischer**

Murals and Trompe l'oeil   106

Leslie Ann Powers   108
European Stenciling, Trompe l'oeil & Murals

Julie Sims Messenger   116
Art Floorcloths

Mary Jo O'Hearn   124

Patti Bruce   132
Patti Bruce Decorative Art

James Alan Smith   138
Decorative Hand Painting

Warnock Studios   146
Fine Surface Decoration

Directory   154

About the Author   160

Introduction

NESTING IS INSTINCTUAL. MOST SPECIES BUILD NESTS AS SHELTERS. HOME to the human species, however, is meant to be more than a simple shelter. Home is a sanctuary; and a sanctuary is meant to be calm and peaceful, balanced and beautiful. Some believe that the psychological health and wellbeing of human beings depends on it.

Sophisticated Surfaces is designed to inspire readers to view their homes as more than mere protection from the elements. It is about applying paint imaginatively to create aesthetically pleasing environments. *Sophisticated Surfaces* is about beauty and harmony. It is about encouraging readers to view ordinary living space in new, extraordinary ways. Home, then, is a nest with an eye toward aesthetics, a shelter uniquely composed to satisfy practical needs while, at the same time, nourishing the soul.

Sophisticated Surfaces is divided into three sections: **Faux and Fantasy Finishes; Painted Surfaces;** and **Murals and Trompe l'oeil.** Each section focuses on work by decorative artists who excel in what we call the "art of transformation." Using readily available materials, each artist translates the ordinary into the extraordinary. Approaches vary with each artist and range from deceptively simple applications of paint to complex multi-layered techniques.

Decorative artists are concerned with shape and form, color and texture in much the same way as fine artists. The primary difference, perhaps, is size. More often than not, decorative artists think and work on a

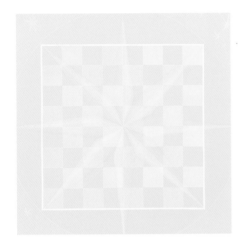

very large scale. The three-dimensional aspect of the world of decorative artists adds a rich texture to their aesthetic considerations. The "viewer" of decorative art is also a "participant," interacting freely with the totality of the environment. Decorative artists must create with this in mind. Additionally, they must remain sensitive to the existing environment—fabrics, window treatments, and accessories. Often, the artist's palette is influenced by certain "givens." Their tools, however, are deceptively simple and certainly unorthodox—ripped rags, crumpled newsprint, sponges, brushes, and the like.

Sophisticated Surfaces is not about teaching readers how to execute precise techniques. It is about encouraging readers to view their living space with a fresh eye; to appreciate the value of living in harmony with their environment; to experiment, perhaps, but more importantly, to come to fully appreciate home as the sanctuary it is.

Karen Aude

Photos: (opposite) courtesy of Ellen Lemer Korney; (this page, top) James M. Goodnough Photography; (this page, bottom) courtesy of Warnock Studios

Sin ser faro ni roca
I AM NOT A LIGHTHOUSE OR A ROCK,
En medio del mar estoy,
BUT I LIVE AT THE END OF THE SEA,
También estoy en la playa:
YOU'LL ALSO FIND ME IN THE SAND—
¡Adivinen, pues, quién soy!
NOW GUESS WHO I MIGHT BE.

Un Caracol – a Seashell

Faux and Fantasy Finishes

Painting surfaces is not a new idea—even prehistoric people painted images on cave walls. Modern techniques, however, are rooted in traditions shaped during the Italian Renaissance in fifteenth-century Europe, painted traditions emulated and expanded upon to this day.

Contemporary American decorative artists use modern tools and materials to interpret age-old techniques—marbleizing, graining, glazing, and the like. Today's artists, however, move beyond traditional methods to create fantasy finishes and textures—cracked linens and textured wall surfaces among them. At times, the end result references natural materials; at times the finished surface captures pure fantasy.

In the following section, you'll find an example of very traditional faux bois rosewood, meticulously painted by the artists to imitate the richness of natural rosewood. By contrast, you'll also appreciate surface treatments inspired by color and texture, conceptual ideas rendered by the artist with honesty and integrity.

Bopas

Tradition and craftsmanship characterize sophisticated painted finishes by Gedes Paskauskas and Robert Grady, partners in Bopas Studio in Boston, Massachusetts. Graduates of the School of the Worcester Art Museum, the partners apply their in-depth knowledge of color theory and application of pigment to their trade as decorative artists. Exquisite finishes unique to Bopas result. There is a natural translucence to their work, a richness that reveals itself through layers of skillfully applied paints and varnishes. This is especially apparent in their innovative rendering of standard wall and wood finishes. "Our inspiration comes from the beauty of the wood or material we're trying to recreate," says Grady, who understands that the most successful techniques are understated. The objective is to harmonize, not compete, with other elements in the room. Bopas employs six full-time artists, each trained in the fine arts. Paskauskas and Grady believe this distinction accounts for the inspired application of painted finishes for which Bopas is known.

Facing page:

Detail, Faux Bois Library

A soft sheen reminiscent of polished natural rosewood harmonizes with hand-painted Chinese wall murals and helps to create a mood of elegance.

Photos by Bruce T. Martin

Several layers of paint and varnish were applied to achieve graining characteristics of natural rosewood. In the darkest sections, intense markings flow back and forth; light and dark areas line up in a staccato fashion with areas of deep amber glowing through to the surface.

PASKAUSKAS AND GRADY PREPARE THE EXISTING MAHOGANY AND poplar surfaces by applying a base coat of an intense amber color. The amber glows through each succeeding layer of varnish and replicates the natural glow of exotic, high-quality rosewood. With their training as fine artists, the partners understand how to manipulate color, value, and line to reproduce a natural grained effect with oil paints, artist colors, and varnishes.

The partners were responsible for all the finishes here, from graining bookshelves, crown molding, chair rail, wainscoting, audiovisual built-in unit, and mantle, to glazing the ceiling and gilding details. They chose a ragging treatment for the ceiling, glazing the entire surface in a celadon green. The subtle yellowish-green tones of the celadon complement the soft amber glow of the rosewood, polished to a satiny sheen with a mixture of rotten stone and oil. To create this harmonious whole, the artists were inspired by the natural qualities of exotic rosewood and by fabrics and hand-painted Chinese wall murals chosen by the designer.

Maintaining the tonal consistency of faux bois is a challenge when applying the painted finish to several surfaces in one room. This audio-visual unit plus bookshelves, moldings, chair rail, wainscoting, and mantle are rendered in faux bois rosewood.

1

Faux Bois Rosewood
Paskauskas and Grady achieve the warm glow and distinctive markings of rosewood through skillful manipulation of glazes and painstaking attention to detail.

Photos, this page by Bruce T. Martin

2
Deep amber is the base color of faux bois rosewood by Bopas.

3
The artists apply custom-mixed glazes—a combination of Vandyke brown and black artist colors—to lay in the overall patterning of the grain.

4
Using a small sable brush, the artists articulate the characteristics of rosewood's distinctive graining.

A Gallery of Surfaces by Bopas

As artists, we enjoy the challenge of developing a wall finish that first uses color to set off the objects in the room, and then uses a textural motif to animate the surface.

Gedes Paskauskas and Robert Grady

"Tuscany" Wall Mural
Inspired by Tuscan gardens, Paskauskas and Grady use acrylic wall paints and artist colors to render this mural, measuring 11.5 feet by 14 feet (3.5 meters by 4.3 meters). Blue sky completes the illusion of indoor/outdoor, activating a plain windowless wall.

***Detail*, "Tuscany" Wall Mural**
A tiny painted butterfly flits on the painted surface, lending reality to illusion.

***Detail*, "Tuscany" Wall Mural**
A plaster cast replica of a Michelangelo sculpture is inspiration for the artists' realistic detailing. With the exception of the chair rail 30 inches (76 centimeters) from the floor, the entire wall surface is painted by Bopas.

Photos, this page by Daniel McManus Photography

Striped Walls

Using a base coat of creamy off-white, Paskauskas and Grady stripe the walls using a vibrant yellow glaze, transforming a dark narrow hallway into a bright sunny area.

Photos, this page by Daniel McManus Photography

Detail, Striped Walls

To stripe the walls, the artists first apply the background color of creamy off-white, then tape the walls, and finally use a brush to glaze the now-isolated stripes.

Sitting Room

Reminiscent of Chinese Tea Paper, this beautifully subtle wall treatment is rendered by a "resist" method unique to Bopas. Glazing a pale yellow/ocher over a pale yellow base, Paskauskas presses lace saturated with solvent into semi-dry glaze. After manipulating the surface, he pulls the fabric away to reveal a series of distinctive impressions.

Photo by Sam Gray Photography
Design by Susan Neddich

Detail, Sitting Room

The "resist" method developed by Paskauskas and Grady effectively mimics the look of Chinese Tea Paper and introduces a softness to their painted surfaces.

Photo courtesy of Bopas

Facing page:

Garden Room

Drawing inspiration from early nineteenth-century itinerant painters, the artists apply their palette of "dirty" colors—yellow ochers, gray greens, burnt oranges—to render this garden room with faded florals and stucco-like wall surface darkened with age.

Photo by Bruce T. Martin

High Victorian Wall Treatment

Paskauskas and Grady painstakingly apply hunter green and ocher glazes to the detailing on the existing plaster relief walls, replicating the original Victorian era wall covering.

Photos, this page by Daniel McManus Photography

***Detail,* High Victorian Wall Treatment**

Pomegranate detailing is evident on this relief plaster wall surface recreated in original colors by the artists.

Welcome Little One, a World of LOVE awaits you here.

Sin ser faro ni roca
I AM NOT A LIGHTHOUSE OR A ROCK
En medio del mar estoy,
BUT I LIVE AT THE END OF THE SEA.
También estoy en la playa:
YOU'LL ALSO FIND ME IN THE SAND.
¡Adivinen, pues, quien soy!
NOW GUESS WHO I MIGHT BE.
Un Caracol ~ a Seashell

Gabriela Sophia's Room

To render the look of eighteenth-century parchment, the artist emphasizes the need for perfection when applying the background color of linen white. Glazes are unforgiving and will reveal any flaws in the initial preparation.

Charlene
Ayuso Cooper

Reflecting on her career as decorative artist, Charlene ("Charley") Ayuso Cooper credits innate artistic talent and independent, focused research into painted finishes as keys to her success. From her experimentation with simple Amish painting methods—stamping surfaces with sliced potatoes dipped in vegetable dye—to rendering sophisticated faux finishes using contemporary methods, Cooper's twelve-year process is extraordinary.

Today, she is the principal in FAUXFinish Studio Inc. located in San Ramon, California. She specializes in European wall glazes, trompe l'oeil, faux stone and marble, woodgraining, and traditional gilding on walls, floors, and furniture. Her technically precise work is balanced with her spontaneous creative expression, and translates nicely into exquisitely rendered painted surfaces. The most successfully executed treatments are ones, she says, "where you can't find where the painted finish starts and where it ends."

***Detail*, Gabriela Sophia's Room**
Cooper designed banners and poems on the walls—written in Spanish and translated into English—to speak to the importance of her family's cultural heritage.

I WANTED TO CREATE AN ENVIRONMENT FOR MY DAUGHTER, Gabriela Sophia, that would be peaceful, calm, and soothing, and also one that would reflect our Spanish heritage. I chose an eighteenth-century parchment finish for the walls, overglazing a custom-mixed celedon-green glaze over a base coat of linen white paint. Celedon is a calming color.

Rolling the glaze onto the walls, I worked in sections measuring 2 feet by 2 feet (60 centimeters by 60 centimeters), manipulating the surface with a piece of glaze-saturated cheesecloth. Working quickly, I flounced and pounded the area with dry cheesecloth, using a wrist motion similar to waving goodbye. This process opened up areas to reveal some of the background color. That's what gives the finish its depth.

I purposefully shied away from themes that might prematurely date the room—Mickey Mouse or Pooh Bear, for example—and I decided on an ocean motif featuring seashells and starfish. I designed what I call my "Pompeii Wave" as a wall frieze, and used raw umber and bronzes with a tinge of green to give the feeling of antiquity.

All photos by Isaac Bailey Photography

A Gallery of Surfaces by Charlene Ayuso Cooper

Chandelier with Hand-painted Vines

The artist renders trompe l'oeil grape vines in fresco style by fading back pigment and sanding the edges to lend a feeling of antiquity.

Interior design by Marjorie Wallace

Bureau with Faux Marble Surface

Cooper updates this 1960s Bombay nightstand by finishing the top in a faux Travertine marble. She completes the look by gold whitewashing the handles and rubbing gold leaf accents onto the sides and bottom.

I seek beauty

through

color,

depth,

and movement.

Charlene Ayuso Cooper

***Detail,* Bureau with Faux Marble Surface**

Applying glazes with tissue paper and finessing with a dry brush, the artist creates her faux Travertine marble.

Dining Room with glazed walls and ceiling
To achieve the deep red, velvety look for these dining room walls and ceiling, the artist uses a traditional milk-based Williamsburg red Casein glaze tinted with raw umber. To seal the water-soluble pigments, she applies a mixture of thinner and oil.

Detail, **Dining Room with glazed walls and ceiling**
Unable to find the desired depth of reds in manufactured paints, the artist rediscovers the rich, honest colors in traditional milk-based paints that she applies with cheesecloth to achieve a deep velvety finish.

Faux Marble Fireplace with Columns

Applying glazes with tissue paper and plastic bags,
Cooper transforms an ordinary plaster fireplace into an
extraordinary faux Roman Travertine marble with
accents of faux black onyx on columns.

Detail, **Faux Marble Fireplace with Columns**
Cooper brushes liquid gold leaf accents to
frame her faux black onyx columns.

Dining Room: Pearlescent Finish

To achieve this contemporary Pearlescent finish, Cooper uses a brush to apply metallic copper drifts as a dramatic contrast to tea-rose and doe-skin background colors. She applies a pearl-white glaze tinted with silver, using glaze-saturated cheesecloth. To finish, she manipulates the edges with dry cheesecloth, and brushes lightly with a dry brush.

Interior design by Marjorie Wallace

Armoire

A faux iron trellis textured with metallic paints offsets
the grey-hued parchment finish of this painted 7-foot
(2.1-meter) armoire.

Detail, **Armoire**

Faux malachite cabinet doors with gold leaf inlay are
the accent for this painted armoire.

Staircase with Ragged Wall

This eighteenth-century parchment treatment in oxblood red is particularly effective. The artist achieves the finish by applying glazes with rollers and cheesecloth, finessing with a dry brush.

Bathroom: Contemporary Metallic Mottle

Cooper excels in contemporary finishes. This she renders in coppers, golds, teals, and purples. She applies paint with a 2-inch (5-centimeter) chip brush using a hand motion similar to French braiding. She then gradates the colors by dabbing the surface with a damp cheesecloth to break up any residue of distinct patterning.

Interior design by Marjorie Wallace

Jeff Entner

Jeff Entner's arts education began in earnest twenty-two years ago; this year marks his ninth working with clients and designers on the exclusive island of Martha's Vineyard off the coast of Massachusetts.

Entner's work reflects the simplicity of island life and the eclectic tastes of its residents, as well as his own creative interpretations. His finishes illustrate the effectiveness of the adage: less is more. His work is charmingly unpretentious. Referencing early folk art techniques, his faux graining is naive yet effective. His skill in applying transformative color washes is superb.

Antiquity interests this island artist, who finds inspiration by looking at old, worn book covers and studying early painted furniture patinaed with age. Entner is a contemporary artist in the tradition of early American itinerant artists—with the exception that Jeff Entner enjoys the luxury of staying on island.

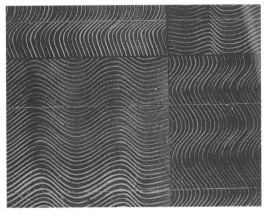

Detail, **Farmhouse: Grained Kitchen Floor "Tiles"**
To achieve the desired depth of color, Entner combs an Indian Red glaze over a salmon-based ground. He then applies three coats of polyurethane to protect the surface.

THE DECORATIVE STYLE OF THIS LATE 1800S FARMHOUSE IS naive; whole floors are spattered and combed. It was important that we respect the integrity of this early styling. Together the New York decorators, the client, and I decided that a primitive graining technique would be appropriate in the renovated kitchen area as well as the stairs leading to the second-floor bedrooms.

To prepare the floor, I applied a salmon-colored base coat, then measured and drew out the squares. In order to achieve the desired effect, I made my own combing tool by cutting irregular notches into a rubber squeegee. I then rolled a glaze of Indian Red over the salmon-colored base, working in small segments at a time. I combed each individual square in a different direction, alternating tile-by-tile. The process was time-consuming. This kitchen is large, which makes the overall effect of the combed tiles more dramatic and extremely effective when viewed as a whole. Interestingly, the whole process is very much like decorative techniques done generations ago by artists combing freshly painted surfaces with ears of dried corn.

Facing page:
Farmhouse: Grained Kitchen Floor "Tiles"
To execute the primitive graining techniques appropriate for this late nineteenth-century farmhouse, the artist measures out kitchen floor "tiles," combing each in a different direction.

Photos by Peter Simon Photography

Hallway: Grained Floor "Tiles"

Maintaining the integrity of style evident in the late
nineteenth-century farmhouse, Entner extends the
combed kitchen floor tiles through to the hallway and up
the stairs to the master bedroom. Complementing the floor
treatment, Entner paints wall stripes freehand to eliminate
sharp edges and remain true to the simplicity of earlier
painting techniques.

Photo by Peter Simon Photography

A Gallery of Surfaces by
Jeff Entner

I see colors in the landscape and

sea; I study how colors go

together, values and hues we

might not even think to use

together. Nature is my inspiration.

Jeff Entner

Detail, Kitchen/Family Room
With accents of salmon, Entner rags the columns using colors complementary to both kitchen and family room, resulting in a unified whole.

Kitchen/Family Room
In the kitchen, Entner rags a blue glaze over a white base; in the family room, he applies a soft, brown glaze over yellow.
Photo by Sauson Luongo

Bathroom

To add a textural interest to the finished wall surface, the artist uses sweeping brushstrokes as he applies the midnight blue glaze to bathroom walls.

Detail, **Bathroom**

To achieve the textural effect of his glazing, Entner uses very visible brushstrokes.

Photos, this page by Sauson Luongo

Conservatory Room: Aged Brick
Entner's whitewashing technique defies viewers
to find the "new" in the "old" brick.

Conservatory Room: Aged Brick
Using paint and illusion, Entner transforms the imposing
fireplace and hearth from unattractive new material into
aged brick.

Photos, this page by Peter Simon Photography

After taping the background wall color, the artist applies denim-blue glazes with a wide stippling brush, a technique which results in calculated irregularities that add interest to the completed striped surfaces.

Photo by Sauson Luongo

To achieve the depth of color, Entner applies two layers of glaze over a base of Navaho White, manipulating each layer with tissue paper to effect a tightly ragged impression. He rags the striping a third time to achieve a deeper version of the glazed wall.

Photo by Peter Simon Photography

Kitchen: Grained Floor "Tiles"

Pulling his notched squeegee twice—in two different directions—over each green-glazed "tile," Entner achieves a woven effect suggestive of a rattan mat.

Photos by Peter Simon Photography

***Detail,* Kitchen Floor: Primitive Graining**

Room angles often interfere with the smooth combing of floor "tiles." One way to deal with challenge is to paint a border around the room, framing in the decorative work.

Joe Fenzl

Twenty years of experience in Santa Monica, California place Joe Fenzl in the forefront of a field that he describes as "a combination of art and craft." Fenzl accurately describes his own exquisitely crafted, painterly decorative techniques. Much of his success is rooted in his knowledge of materials. "If you're not using the correct materials," he says, "you might get a particular finish, but it might not hold up."

Fenzl's color choice and the way in which he approaches his textural finishes reveal his classic sensibilities. He wants his work to fit into the contemporary world yet "remain in style," he says.

Fenzl demonstrates his expertise by using a wide variety of surface materials in creative ways. Always adding to his repertoire, he continually tries new techniques. His series of textural papers for walls is one of Fenzl's innovative contributions to the field of contemporary decorative arts.

***Detail*, Column, Kitchen Breakfast Bar**
Using the same process as with the breakfast bar wall, Fenzl glazes and seals the cement column, transforming an otherwise unattractive detail into a stunningly simple architectural element.

MY CHALLENGE WAS TO CREATE HARMONY IN THIS CALIFORNIA beach condo. Its small size—only 1,200 square feet (108 square meters)—added to the challenge, as did the way in which wall surfaces visually interconnected. The client wanted a contemporary look. To comply, I rendered existing concrete and wood surfaces in soft, textural finishes. I borrowed my palette from nature—muted earth tones, taupe, caramel colors and wood tones—and, playing off the views of sky and sea, I chose muted aqua as an accent color.

Moving from the central kitchen through to the living room, which is separated only by a breakfast bar, and down a short hallway to the master bath, I rendered several complementary surface finishes. In effect, the walls became an unobtrusive backdrop for a condo with spectacular views of the Pacific Ocean—I saw no need to compete with Mother Nature.

Facing page:
Kitchen Breakfast Bar
The concrete wall forming the base of the breakfast bar, and separating kitchen from living room, provides Fenzl with a challenge, which he meets with characteristic aplomb. The artist applies a very, very light aqua glaze to a smooth top layer of cement to achieve an unobtrusive mottled effect..

Photos by Dan Fenzl

Door: Faux Bois, Teak

To contrast with a baseboard of light natural teak wood, Fenzl renders all condo doors in a dark teak faux bois by combing glazes over a medium tan painted ground. A clear glaze tinted with a brown aniline dye simulates the depth of actual teakwood.

Living Room Wall: Distressed Textural Stria

The artist drags a dry brush through a wet acrylic textural paste, which he applies to the wall surface in four-foot wide sections. An application of deerskin taupe glaze followed by a glaze of golden rust accents the stria effect of the brushstrokes.

Photos by Dan Fenzl

Master Bath: Polished Plaster Marble Lustro finish

Tinting Marble Lustro with an earthy taupe, Fenzl trowels his textural wall formula on the walls. After smooth troweling a second layer tinted linen-white, he uses fine steel wool to apply a mixture of beeswax and carnuba wax, which he buffs to a satin sheen. The double layer of Marble Lustro, in complementary pigments, gives the depth of coloration.

A Gallery of Surfaces by Joe Fenzl

Many things influence me. . . .

Nature inspires many of my

textures and surfaces—stones,

the barks of trees. And European

antiquity—old worn plasters

patinaed with age. . . .

Joe Fenzl

Kitchen Cupboard

The artist interprets a look of Italian Tuscany by painting several layers of bone white over a dark stain, sanding back through the layers, and applying an umber finish glaze. Random water marking, a technique whereby fast-drying solvent is spattered sparingly onto the finished piece, adds subtle nuances. Highlighting edges with an oil colorant tinted with raw umber, he clear coats to finish.

Textural Papers for Wall Surfaces

In creating his series of textural papers for wall surfaces, Fenzl uses processes similar to decorative techniques he developed for direct application of materials onto walls. For ease of rolling and subsequent application of his exquisitely rendered, custom-designed, handmade wallpapers to a wall, he builds his textural surfaces using only flexible materials.

Bottom this page and facing page top:

"Ceramic"

Onto white butcher paper, the artist applies a thin layer of acrylic textural material tinted caramel. He then applies a crackle medium to create the eggshell texture. Next, a caramel glaze establishes a soft alabaster color which is finished with a clear coat.

"Stone"

Onto kraft paper, the artist trowels two layers of a textural acrylic—the first tinted gray, the second tinted cream. A final glazing with umber gives the textured paper its canyon color.

Photos by Dan Fenzl

"Frottage"

After applying white paint to butcher paper, Fenzl brushes the surface with glue. When dry, he applies mossy green water-base paint, which reacts with the water soluble glue to create a crackle finish. He then manipulates the wet paint, exposing the background randomly. A raw umber finish glaze creates the patina.

"Porcelain"

With a base of butcher paper, Fenzl randomly trowels on a layer of Marble Lustro, a semi-translucent textural material developed by the artist. A charcoal-colored glaze applied after the crackle medium creates the Raku color of the final paper.

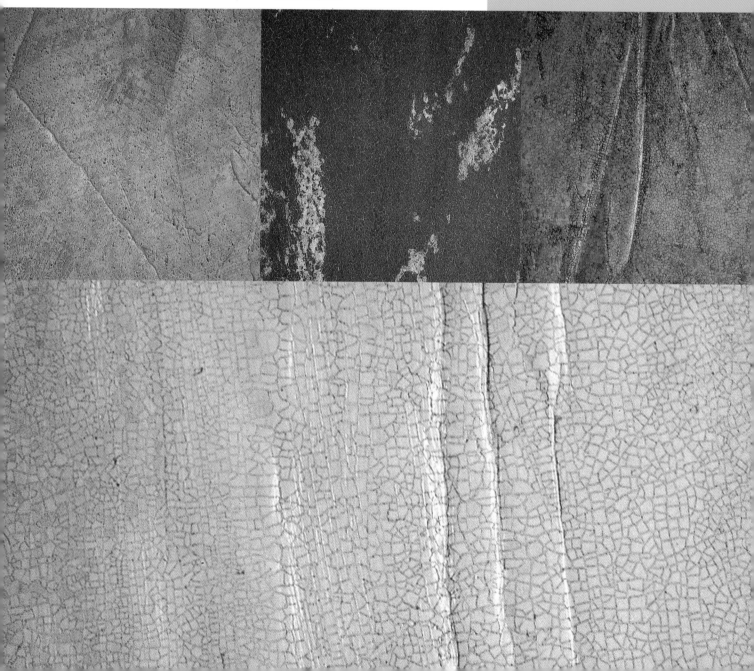

"Leather"

By gluing tissue paper onto kraft paper, the artist creates a wrinkled-up surface similar in appearance to coarse leathers. He paints the textural surface cream, glazes in tan, and establishes an overall tonal quality called "Bombay" by applying a clear finish coat tinted slightly with brown aniline dye.

"Strata"

The artist trowels two layers of acrylic textural material onto kraft paper, the first tinted light charcoal, and the second tinted antique white. Two layers of glazes follow, one peach and the other a charcoal gray. Vertical application of materials contributes to the stone-like effect of the bison-colored surface.

"Antique Gold"

Fenzl applies a thick layer of acrylic textural material to wrinkle the kraft paper base. After applying gold leaf, he partially paints the surface with a thin layer of taupe acrylic. When dry, he glazes the surface and finishes it with a clear coat, water-based acrylic tinted with an earthy brown aniline dye, which gives it its antique gold finish.

"Block" Wall

Fenzl stiples his brush across wet plaster to achieve pitted areas similar to the textures of natural travertine. Simultaneously, the entire surface is scored into blocks. To achieve his desired palette, he glazes a background of light cream in sand tones.

Photo by Chris Covey

Interior design, this page and facing by Ellen Lemer Korney

Facing page:

Pool House

Recreating a Pompeii distressed plaster, the artist applies a coat of drywall compound to the walls. He then rubs pigment into the compound, sanding back randomly and sealing with shellac. His palette is Italian-ocher, chrome green, and Pompeii red with a black band to accent.

Photo courtesy of Ellen Lemer Korney

Dining Room

Manipulating layers of glazes over the patterning of existing English embossed Anaglypta wall, artist Martin Alan Hirsch imitates the look and feel of hand-tooled old world metal.

Martin Alan Hirsch

Martin Alan Hirsch comes to decorative painting with a background in psychology from the University of Alabama. He describes a chance encounter with a work of decorative art as a defining moment in his life. "It was an elevator door painted to look like solid mahogany," he remembers. "As soon as I saw it, something clicked."

The rest is history. Having studied in-depth the art of faux techniques, Hirsch concentrates specifically on surface finishes, using modern materials in creative ways to imitate not only the look of any given material, but also its texture and feel. Thus, for example, Hirsch's faux marble not only looks like marble, it feels like marble and is cool to the touch.

Hirsch owns and operates Decorative Finishes Studio in Louisville, Kentucky. His studio includes a school where the artist shares his knowledge generously, teaching decorative surface finishes to a new generation of decorative artists.

Detail, **Dining Room**
Overglazing the existing English embossed wallcovering with several layers of glazes mixed with 22-carat gold powder, Hirsch achieves the look and feel of hand-tooled metal on the wall surfaces in his client's dining room.

OUR CHARGE AND OUR CHALLENGE IN THIS DINING ROOM was to take the existing embossed English wall covering and make it look like hand-tooled metal. To accomplish this, we applied four layers of glazes beginning with cobalt blue and finishing with shades of green golds to effect a patinaed metal finish. We achieved the gold cast by actually mixing 22-carat gold powders into the glazes before application. We used cheesecloth and badger brushes to blend the glazes, working the gold into the recesses, rubbing off random surface areas, and giving a verde feel to the surface without reproducing the actual distress and deterioration of a verde finish. To complete the visual illusion, we covered the whole surface with a satin lacquer. This also added the tactile element, giving the feel of metal to the painted surface. The final effect is exquisite in its simple elegance. Not wanting other elements in the room to compete, we decided to treat the ceiling and trim as a simple frame, and so we brushed both with a gold powder finish by, again, adding 22-carat gold powder to the glaze. This time, however, we sprayed the entire ceiling and trim surfaces with a solid covering. A final overglaze in umber added the aged patina.

Foyer

The artist renders the foyer walls using the same technique as developed for the adjacent dining room, adding 22-carat gold powder to his glazes before brushing over a solid base coat of cobalt blue. He then pounces the surface lightly with cheesecloth to give it the soft glowing look.

A Gallery of Surfaces by
Martin Alan Hirsch

My motto is 'bridging the gap

between reality and illusion.' To

accomplish this, I am inspired by

antiquity and all the things I see on

my many trips overseas, mainly to

Italy and most often to Venice.

Martin Alan Hirsch

Library Ceiling
Soaking an old black and white map in water, the artist
applies the softened sheet to a wet ceiling. He then seals,
colors, and ages the surface to create the look of antiquity.

***Detail,* Library Ceiling**
After creating a thick, textured surface imitating old
chipped plaster, the artist physically colors lettering
and land masses.

Detail, Fireplace Wall

Painting each of the eleven layers of drywall individually, the artist chips and peels away the surface to reveal layers of subtle colorations.

Fireplace Wall

Texture is key in much of Hirsch's work. Here, the artist re-creates the look and feel of an ancient and deteriorating castle wall. He builds the wall surface with eleven layers of drywall, mortar, cement, and plaster.

Foyer

Rendering the walls in a three-step fresco finish using a palette of raw umber, black, and taupe, Hirsch frames his composition with faux marble crown molding.

Detail, **Foyer Trim**

Hirsch frames the foyer walls by rendering crown molding in an imitation Rasotica, a Yugoslavian marble that is composed of black and brown fossil shells.

Den

Brushing burgundy, earth green and Italian sienna glazes onto hand-plastered walls prepared with an off-white background, Hirsch creates the look of old Tuscan plaster.

***Detail,* Dining Room**

The wall surfaces in the dining room and foyer are a faux fresco in shades of coral. Using chemicals to affect the glazes, the artist achieves a surface that looks textured but is actually smooth.

Below right and above:

Dining Room

Hirsch achieves the textured look of worn fresco by using a "reactive" finish. He begins with a coral base, over which he manipulates layers of glazes by applying chemicals to give a calcified appearance.

Dining Room

Building columns from drywall, Hirsch paints the surface to simulate an Italian marble, solidifying the illusion by adding sand to the glaze, which he uses to paint grout lines. Hirsch renders the dining room walls in an Old World parchment finish, applying two layers of glazes with cheesecloth and brushes.

Painted Surfaces

The history of modern painted furniture parallels the history of faux finishes, periods of artistic experimentation focusing on interior decor. The aesthetic sensibility that appreciated the fine art of painted furniture continues to evolve as artists boldly encourage clients to experiment with their environments.

In Europe, elaborately painted furniture in the courts and palaces of the nobility made its appearance three centuries ago. Initially the artist's intent was to imitate natural materials, an extension of the faux finishes applied to wall surfaces and architectural detailing. Later, the furniture became something of a three-dimensional canvas onto which artists painted scenes and decorations. Oriental lacquered furniture first made its appearance when Europe and America began trade with the Far East. These elaborately and exquisitely painted and gilded pieces of furniture had an enormous influence on generations of artists and crafts-people in the West.

Today, anything goes. In this section, you will find artists engaged in executing a variety of methods and approaches from painting furniture to complement fabric, to simulating marble on a fireplace hearth.

Photos: (background) James M. Goodnough Photography; (clockwise from top) Jim Stob Photographer; Jim Stob Photographer; Vince Valdez; James M. Goodnough Photography; Kelli Ruggere Photography; James M. Goodnough Photography

Dining Room Table

Adding a wide whitewashed stripe and hand-painted woodbine leaves and currant-colored berries to a simple pine table, the artists borrow their palette from the chair coverings. For consistency, the artists carry the design onto the dining chairs.

Photo by James M. Goodnough Photography

Dale Wade and Helen Doane

Cape Cod, Massachusetts artists Dale Wade and Helen Doane combine their talents, sometimes working together, sometimes individually. It all depends on individual client needs and the complexity and size of a commission. The two women credit a trompe l'oeil class taught by the late Heather Braginton-Smith, a talented artist and gifted teacher, as the defining moment in the development of their decorative arts career.

Wade and Doane share many skills, an ability to simplify being one. This is most apparent when the artists coordinate painted finishes with existing design elements, fabrics in particular. Rather than reproducing draperies, upholstery, or bed linen designs in what can be distracting detail, Wade's and Doane's painted surfaces complement existing fabrics. Additionally, the artists share a sophisticated sense of color, critical to matching paints to dyes. After almost a decade in business, Wade and Doane render faux finishes and trompe l'oeil techniques in addition to decorative painting.

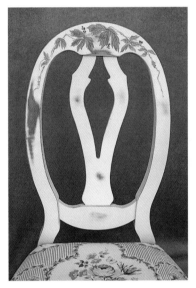

Dining Room Chair
In a simple yet effective gesture, the artists add decorative designs to the back of production-line dining chairs, pulling their palette from the seat coverings.
Photo by Dale Michaels Wade

WE'VE FOUND SUCCESSFUL DECORATIVE PAINTING DOESN'T mean covering an entire surface with paint. This pine dining table, with its wide whitewashed striped and hand-painted woodbine leaves and currant-colored berries, illustrates the elegance of simplicity.

Our greatest challenge with this project was to find an innovative way to expand the seating capacity of this dining table from six to ten. Our solution was to build a "topper," or "tabletop mural" that would hang on the dining room wall until needed. We decided to paint a local scene, working from our original photograph. Then we painted trompe l'oeil window mullions and draperies to complete the illusion. Until pressed into action, the topper hangs behind the dining table and provides a "view" to the outside world.

Dining Room Table "Topper"

Painting from an original photograph of a local scene, the artists view the "topper" as a huge "canvas." Trompe l'oeil window mullions and draperies complete the illusion. Until pressed into action, the topper hangs behind the dining table and provides a "view" to the outside world.

Photo by Dale Michaels Wade

A Gallery of Surfaces by Dale Wade and Helen Doane

Each project presents unique challenges. We're inspired by several things—our customers' objectives, the final function of the piece or space in which we're working, tangible influences such as fabric and architecture, together with our two separate artistic sensibilities working together.

Dale Wade and Helen Doane

Detail, Room Screen
Wade paints a bronze-colored fence to create dimension on the three-paneled room divider. She adds vines using a combination of hand painting and stenciling.

Room Screen
Combining hand painting and stenciling, Wade paints a room divider screen with a turn-of-the century English block print design inspired by antique wallpaper.

Photos, this page by James M. Goodnough Photography

Game Table, Fishing Theme

Doane confines herself to single themes when painting decorative game tables. Here, a fishing theme features "sand," fishing nets, bits of seaweed, a broken crab claw, mussel and scallop shells, and a fish hook "caught" in the net.

Photos, right and below left by James M. Goodnough Photography

Game Table, Nautical Theme

A compass rose, painted in shades of cerulean and indigo, adds sparks of deep color. In keeping with a celestial motif and complementing the room's nautical theme, Doane paints gold stars around the edge of the game table.

Game Table, Hunting Theme

Wade paints a faux leather border in a rich burgundy color. Corner detailings accentuate the hunting theme.

Photo by Dale Michaels Wade

***Detail,* Pedestal Table**

Doane borrows her palette, styling, and use of gold leaf from motifs popularized during the China Trade of the ninteenth century.

Bedroom Furniture

Wade accomplishes her cross-combing technique by brushing a bright sunny yellow glaze in one direction, and a soft buttery yellow in another. The overall effect is textural, yet doesn't compete with designs that Wade adds to her surface finishes—blue ribbon entwined with seaform green leaves on the game table, lattice panels on the armoire.

Pedestal Table

Doane renders Oriental designs and 23-carat gold leafing in a manner reminiscent of decorative styles prevalent during the China Trade in the early to mid 1800s.

***Detail,* Bedroom Furniture**

When designing the headboard, Wade pulls decorative elements from the other pieces in the room, although she opts to paint them in what she calls a "small print" motif.

Photos, this page by James M. Goodnough Photography

Coffee Table and Tinware

Helen Doane transforms a simple wooden chest into a conversation piece by painting faux brick sides and adding ivy and an exquisite blue butterfly. Doane's hand-painted tin boxes and trays add decorative interest to a cozy corner and provide her client with an instant "collection."

Photos, right and below left by James M. Goodnough Photography

Tray: Nineteenth-century American Toleware design

Doane frames this authentic nineteenth-century American floral design with a 23-carat gold leaf border. The rose, morning glory, and other flowers are common features on Victorian era Toleware, from which Doane borrows her palette and technique.

Floorcloth

Wade transforms a simple cotton canvas into a "goldfish pond" floorcloth.

Photo by Dale Michaels Wade

Detail, Trompe l'oeil Panel

Trompe l'oeil Cabinet

Wade adds a bit of whimsy to a trompe l'oeil panel, rendering a faux bois cabinet featuring fishing lures, books, and paraphernalia, and a very believable photo "taped" to the door.

Photos by James M. Goodnough Photography

Kitchen Bureau

Juxtaposing an imaginative color palette, the artist transforms a large awkward
piece bureau into fine art furniture.

Kathy McDonald

Kathy McDonald thinks back to childhood when she thinks of her first dabblings into painting and decorating. Painting is now woven into the very fabric of her life: today more than ever, considering that McDonald's current challenge is to paint surfaces to match or complement fabrics in a client's home.

A certified decorative artist through the National Society of Toll and Decorative Painters, McDonald's style is joyful and refreshingly simple. She conceals any complexities from her viewers. Delightful decorative finishes and designs result as she juxtaposes her imaginative palette with a playfulness that engages the eye.

The artist's decade-plus-old Chicago business is very much word of mouth. McDonald works for individual clients and through interior designers—which, in fact, she herself is. The dual designation—interior designer/decorative artist—serves her well as she collaborates with clients, helping them to create their own unique environments.

Detail, Kitchen Bureau
The artist paints every square inch of this large kitchen bureau, adding color accents and detailing according to her detailed design sketch.

IN ITS RAW STATE, THIS KITCHEN BUREAU WAS TOO BIG AND TOO unattractive. But I saw it and knew immediately—here was a chance to make a statement.

I clipped pictures from magazines and asked my clients to show me ones that attracted their attention. A "blueprint" of their stylistic preferences and palette developed as they responded to geometries, bright colors, and metallics. With this valuable information in hand, I made a sketch and color board for their approval.

I used creative color combinations—purples, periwinkle, turquoise blues, golds, teals, coppers, and pearlized paints and metallics—to make our design statement. In executing, I penciled or taped individual sections. The inevitable irregularities where I followed pencil lines and painted freehand added to the charm of this piece, which I call "contemporary funk."

Believing details make a difference, I sculpted knobs from clay, pushing little metallic stones into the material when it was still soft. Later I painted them to accent the existing color story. And to add to the illusion of my painted "tiles," I masked off grout lines before I applied the high-gloss polyurethane to the entire piece.

***Detail,* Kitchen Bureau**

To lend an air of authenticity to her painted tiles, the artist tapes grout lines before applying a coat of high-gloss polyurethane to finish.

***Detail,* Kitchen Bureau**

Using pencil lines as guides, the artist paints various sections freehand, a technique that adds to the primitive charm of the piece.

A Gallery of Surfaces by Kathy McDonald

My clients inspire me. I look around

and build on what I see in their homes,

the styles they prefer. . . . I try to

complement and coordinate my style

with theirs. A decorative artist is a

different kind of artist, and it's a

different kind of process.

Kathy McDonald

***Detail,* Kitchen Hutch, knobs**
Using a clay-like craft material, the artist sculpts and
paints drawer knobs in keeping with the playful and
casual ambiance of the piece.

Kitchen Hutch
Painting subtle checks and stripes in butter yellows and apple greens, the
artist transforms an old secondhand kitchen hutch into a work of art. In
keeping with the casual aspects of the piece, McDonald works freehand
from penciled lines.

Detail, Kitchen Border, bird

The artist's interest in detailing is evident with her addition of this exquisitely painted bird, which has ostensibly "escaped" from the open door of the painted bird cage.

Kitchen Border, bird cage

Pulling navy blue and burgundies from fabrics in an adjoining room, the artist renders her freehand painted border design.

Detail, Laundry Room

Concerned about the inevitable moisture in the laundry room, the artist, who works in acrylics, seals her walls and decorative elements with a low-gloss polyurethane.

Laundry Room

Challenged to expand a cramped laundry room space, McDonald invites the outdoors in. There is a certain neoclassic look to the wall treatment with its potted plants and views of English gardens.

Above:

Master Bedroom

Pulling mauves, lilacs, and plums from the existing bedspread, McDonald uses a bath sponge to manipulate four color layers on the walls in the master bedroom.

At top right:

Detailing in Master Bedroom & Master Bath

McDonald adds plaster to the paint to lend depth and texture to the "iron trellis" detailing of her painted woody vine and leaf border design in both the master bedroom and bath.

Master Bath

The master bath wall treatments echo the wall treatment in the adjacent master bedroom.

Detail, Dining Room columns

Accenting the architectural detailing on existing columns, the artist applies washes of purples and greens, which she then rubs back randomly. She achieves the final aged patina by brushing an antique wash over all surfaces.

Dining Room

Taking her palette from existing wallpaper, the artist sponges the dining room walls with soft finish reminiscent of old Italian plaster. Painted stonework frames the archway, and patinaed columns complement the overall ambiance of the room.

John Parsons

Contemporary decorative artists follow in the footsteps of self-taught, itinerant masters whose ingenious approach to applying paint to surface continues to inspire. John Parsons is one such artist. Refining his painting techniques by trial and error, this New England artist's goal is "to make the room look like a million bucks—with paint." To achieve this lofty objective, Parsons paints "total environments," and says that interpreting space with paint fits his talent and temperament perfectly. He juxtaposes colors imaginatively and uses furniture as form to create wholly integrated design concepts. Parsons' work is delightfully naive in an unpretentious way, with a freshness that is both charming and convincing. He believes simplicity is key. "Often details on a piece of old wooden furniture come alive by applying even just one accent color," he says.

Built-in Bureau
Complementary greens, corals, yellows, and periwinkle edged in dramatic black-and-white painted "tiles" transform an otherwise nondescript built-in bureau into a whimsical accent piece.

OLIVIA'S ROOM, ON THE TOP FLOOR OF A TINY BUNGALOW, IS small and divided in two by a central chimney. Sloped walls complicate the space. The client wanted to transform the attic bedroom into a total environment suitable for her active seven-year-old daughter.

"My greatest challenge was to find a way to incorporate the awkward slope of the walls into my overall design concept," said Parsons. To create the tent-like effect of festooned fabric, Parsons brushed five-inch-wide (13-centimeter) continuous stripes up the walls and over the ceiling using Hancock's Verbena Pink oil-based paint. He then brushed each individual stripe with Hancock's Venetian Rose, a slightly darker color, using a semi-circular hand motion. Because the colors proved to be stronger than his intended outcome, Parsons used a white finish glaze to soften the overall feel. He applied it with a 2.5" (5 cm) dry brush, continuing his semi-circular brushstroke and completing the illusion of "standing inside an Arabian Princess's tent."

The chimney created a natural divide between play and sleeping areas. To visually unite both, Parsons brushed seafoam green paint onto a floorcloth he made from two remnants of linoleum. After consultation with Olivia, he added a few of her favorite things—hearts, stars, squiggly lines, star-fish—using soft, pleasing colors like apple green, coral, pale yellows, powdery blues, and periwinkle.

Facing page:
Olivia's Room
To create the tent-like effect of festooned fabric Parsons brushes continuous stripes up the walls and over the ceiling. "It's like walking into an experience," says Parsons of the room's painted walls, ceiling, floor, and furniture.

Photos by Kelli Ruggere Photography

Armoire "Town House"

This 5-foot (1.5-meter) armoire "Town House" with its painted Palladian windows, wrought iron railings and front stoop is home to Olivia's dolls, thanks to Parsons' imaginative design.

False Drawer Front

Parsons applies playful designs to a false drawer front framed to conceal an air-conditioning unit tucked under the eaves.

Photos by Kelli Ruggere Photography

A Gallery of Surfaces by John Parsons

Much of my inspiration for surfaces comes from nature, flower gardens in particular. They seem so carefully composed, so full of color and balance, yet so natural . . . . so exactly right.

John Parsons

Breakfast Room
Manipulating a pale custom-mixed green wall glaze with cheesecloth, Parsons reproduces the look of old plastered walls. Wisteria vines creep up and out of painted pots and wind around the room to create the ambiance of a light and cheery room.

Detail, Breakfast Room
Parsons achieves a stucco-like effect by manipulating a pale green wall glaze with bunched-up cheesecloth to create a mottled appearance. Wisteria vines are a natural way to carry the garden theme throughout the room, which measures 15 feet by 15 feet (4.6 meters by 4.6 meters).

Painted Vanity

This thrift shop vanity is crackle-finished by Parsons who, in consultation with designer Sandra J. Tuthill, paints the doors with decorative elements borrowed from existing floor tiles. The faux marble top completes the transformation.

Photo above courtesy of Sandra J. Tuthill, ASID

Top:

Painted Credenza

Executing the design concepts of designer Sandra J. Tuthill, Parsons paints an otherwise plain credenza painted to coordinate with fabric and tiled kitchen tabletop from Italy.

Above:

Detail, **Painted Credenza**

Custom mixing colors, Parsons matches his palette to fabrics and imported kitchen tiles.

At left:

Faux Lattice Foyer

Attention to detail is key when rendering trompe l'oeil lattice. After taping walls in the crisscross lattice pattern, Parsons paints the background—sky, water, and coral-colored wisteria that complements an adjoining room. He then removes the tape to reveal the background white wall color in the lattice-work pattern.

Photos by Kelli Ruggere Photography

Trompe l'oeil Mud Room

Parsons paints organized clutter in a trompe l'oeil mud room that never needs straightening!

Jackets belong to the client's sons and Parsons admits, "the patterns were challenging!"

Clock Face Table

Nostalgia and whimsy come together in Parsons'
reproduction antique clock-face table. Trimming edges
with faux bois mahogany, Parsons uses custom-mixed
glazes to age the off-white surface color. He adds black
lettering, hints of brass, and the final touch-—the client's
grandson's name replaces the clockmaker's insignia.

Photos by Kelli Ruggere Photography

Detail, Kitchen Floorcloth

Picking up the yellows, pinks, and greens of his client's china, Parsons coordinates his painted kitchen floorcloth to existing decor. To ensure durability, he finishes the work with six coats of acrylic varnish.

Kitchen Floorcloth

Inspired by existing tile and housewares in the client's kitchen, Parsons custom paints a canvas floorcloth, measuring 4 feet by 4 feet (1.2 meters by 1.2 meters). Working with designer Sandra J. Tuthill, Parsons chooses mottled soft-toned yellows and beiges as background.

English Dressing Room

Murphy achieves the look of Venetian stucco on the dado and pilasters in this English dressing room by tinting a form of plaster and applying it with a palette knife to the surface area. The result is a stone-like surface, which he finishes with a soft sheen.

Michael Tyson Murphy

Michael Tyson Murphy traces his obsession with shape, form, and interior aesthetics to a trip he made to Europe at age fourteen. He retraces the steps guiding him to his current work—first trompe l'oeil painting while in high school, then studies at the San Francisco Art Institute and his stint as assistant to the artist Helen Frankenthaler, and always his own paintings on canvas.

Working from his New York studio, Murphy is part-artist, part-artisan; he is part-architect and part-designer. He is part raconteur, though he tells his stories in paint not words. His choice of subject and complementary styling often reference what he sees on his travels in Europe. "I go in cycles," he explains. "What happens a great deal is that I pick a thing of particular interest to me and become almost obsessed. My elaborate faux bois floors are inspired by eastern Europe; my mosaic painting comes from my experiences in Portugal."

A harmonious integration of the whole best describes Murphy's stylistic approach, which has to do with how he composes all the elements in any given environment. "I adjust a room in the same way I might compose a painting," he explains. "I consider how people will enter the room, where they might sit, what they will see."

Murphy's room compositions are precisely what interiors ought to be—aesthetically integrated and psychologically containing.

All photos by Dennis Krukowski

Detail, **English Dressing Room**

AS WITH ALL MY WORK, I WANTED TO CREATE A DRESSING room in harmony with each of the elements that make up the environment. I wanted to do this in a way that worked with the overall architecture of the space. I composed this room to resemble an English dressing room, very much in a Georgian spirit.

The walls are done in a simple butter-yellow glaze with trompe l'oeil architectural detailing as evidenced by the banding and painted arch, in the center of which I painted a Wedgwood medallion using a very traditional Wedgwood blue. The dado and pilaster offered natural opportunities for gentle contrast. I treated both to simulate marble using Venetian stucco which achieves the feel and luster of real stone.

I often design furniture for the areas in which I work. Here I designed the dressing cabinet with a central panel to accommodate an antique Persian painting owned by my client. I then reproduced smaller patterns in the style of the Persian original, adapting my palette to the color story I had developed for the whole of the interior.

A Russian-inspired faux bois floor completes my composition. Painted to imitate mahogany, ebony, walnut, and cherry, the design radiates from a central point and thus complements, grounds, and integrates all the elements of this room.

A Gallery of Surfaces by
Michael Tyson Murphy

When I look at a space, I absolutely divine my inspiration not only from the client's personal interests but from what the existing architecture will allow. Sometimes the existing architecture says "no," and in my view you have to respect that.

Michael Tyson Murphy

Lady's Bedroom

Murphy articulates the corner decoration in this small bedroom by imitating traditional Portuguese blue and white tiles; he designs trompe l'oeil architecture to connect crown and dado, choosing a golden sandstone palette for the walls. French moss-green accent unites all hand-painted elements. He renders bedside tables in Italian Rococo marquetry with insets of birds and flowering plants, and a faux marble top done in traditional Venetian rose verona. His French-inspired headboard features faux bois satin wood, sandalwood, and ebony with accents of gilding and trompe l'oeil ivory inlay.

Sitting Room off Master Bedroom

Murphy achieves his highly successful faux bois mahogany wall panels by layering glazes tinted from light to darker banana colors and French mustard. Adding interest and age, he stencils an Italian Gothic patterning in green and gold. The accent piece is a faux bois radiator cover accented with gold leafing and mother-of-pearl inlay. Octagonal and interlocking marquetry floor resembles French pavement patterning.

Hall to Master Suite

Murphy stains handmade Belgian linen with tea to effect an even, soft mottle, over which he stencils original Victorian-inspired patterns in a palette of soft violets. His original painting conspires to bring the outdoors in.

Foyer of Apartment

To add depth and activity to the wall surface in the grand foyer, Murphy articulates beveled edge "stone" accentuated by trompe l'oeil pilasters and dado rendered in the same palette of desert rust.

Powder Room

Dusty rose clouds and a sky of peacock blue, azure, and teal form the backdrop for Murphy's tablature rendered in imitation bas relief carved stone on the walls of this small Anglo-Indian powder room.

Faux Bois Foyer

Beginning with a rather dark banana base color, Murphy adds four layers of veining to achieve the illusion of faux bois satin wood on the foyer walls. He then paints a custom-made console table in an elaborate marquetry pattern, which successfully imitates satinwood, ebony, walnut, and fruitwood.

Facing page:
Second Floor Foyer

Murphy renders the walls with a soft grisaille landscape. The top of his custom-made hall table is painted with the floor plan of the fantasy house. Above hang two original paintings by the artist.

Entryway: Cracked Linen Walls and Stenciled Border

Mastroluca's cracked linen technique—made by floating a custom-mixed compound onto linen and then applying the prepared sheets to the designated surface—lends itself nicely to large areas. Using water-soluble glazes, Mastroluca dries and cracks the surface, washes it down, rubs it back, and distresses it to give it a look patinaed with age.

Photo by Vince Valdes
Interior design courtesy of Beacon Hill Showroom

Suzanne Mastroluca

A sophisticated palette informs decorative artwork by Suzanne Mastroluca. It is a very beautiful, very old-world palette, inspired by the dusty, subtle, faded colors of early Italian frescoes.

A corporate dropout, Mastroluca's goal as artist is to "make a worthy contribution to others through my work." Thus she devotes herself not only to perfecting technique, but also to learning about what is important to clients so she can better interpret their needs. "I linger in clients' spaces . . . . Perhaps, for example, there's a painting they love; I try to imagine using those colors."

Dialogue is important to Mastroluca, as is experimentation. Building on traditionally accepted painting techniques, Mastroluca perfects her formula for producing cracked linen surfaces. She renders much of her work using a base product of casein paints, which fade back with water and overglaze beautifully. Painted borders, for which Mastroluca is known, lend themselves nicely to this creative approach.

Detail: **Entryway**

Mastroluca stencils the walls with a very traditional Greek Key border design, using Dutch metal leaf. She applies the gold sizing with a rough rag rather than smooth brush. The leaf adheres in a mottled fashion, in keeping with the worn, faded appearance of the cracked linen walls.

Photo courtesy of the artist

THE SIZE OF THIS ENTRYWAY WAS A CHALLENGE. I WANTED TO keep its grand impact yet introduce a more human scale. My cracked linen technique lent itself nicely to the challenge. It's textural. Using a trowel, I float a handmade compound onto linen, crack it, glaze it, and then attach it to the walls. It's versatile. Once attached, I can overglaze it, wash it down, smudge it, fade it back, distress it. Here, I used a golden ocher glaze, adding some metallic powder for a bit of shimmer.

The border design is a traditional Greek Key stenciled with Dutch metal leaf. I used a rag to apply the gold sizing, so when I stenciled the leaf it adhered in a mottled fashion, thus complementing the patina of the fresco-like walls. To fade it back even more, I applied a tinted varnish, which sealed and discolored it. Like many border designs, this lowers the ceiling which is 16 feet high (4.9 meters) in this room.

In the adjacent room, I striped the walls by taping the surface after I had applied the cracked linen. Using cheesecloth, I softly glazed the open areas of the stripe in taupe. When dry, I pulled the tape off and glazed the entire wall in a lighter taupe. In most cases, I glazed the moldings and doors so they wouldn't be visible. The idea was that the furniture would be the focal point.

A Gallery of Surfaces by
Suzanne Mastroluca

Great Room: Frescoed Walls

Applying casein paints to the walls, Mastroluca's technique imitates aged frescoes. She then paints her flowing, freehand border motif, finishing all surfaces with a transparent terra-cotta glaze to complement the Mediterranean styling in this Great Room with interior decor by Pat Larin.

Photos by John Vaughan, courtesy of the artist

I'm inspired by the architecture elements in the homes in which I work—the corbels, carvings, and friezes. I often borrow line, shape, or form and translate these elements into decorative touches.

Suzanne Mastroluca

Detail, **Great Room: Frescoed Walls**

In places, Mastroluca's hand-painted border dips four feet down, serving to visually lower the height of the ceiling.

Border Designs

Border Design

Applying layers of subtly shaded Etruscan brick-red translucent glazes, the artist achieves the rich depths in her cracked linen border. Stylized leaves are added last, then sanded back before the final glazing with raw umber.

Detail, Border Design

Hand-painted border by Mastroluca features Acanthus leaves and grapes typical of early Greek decorative motifs. The border is cracked linen, rubbed back and faded with transparent glazes.

Border Design

Mastroluca paints her handmade cracked linen panels with a background of parchment white, and adds her floral motif which she then sands and overglazes using her signature technique.

Trompe l'oeil "Grapes Carved in Stone"

Borrowing elements of her design from a wine label, Mastroluca paints her trompe l'oeil "Grapes Carved in Stone" on the wall of a wine cellar.

Photos by John Vaughan, courtesy of the artist

Trompe l'oeil Windows and Shutters

It's no matter that these windows and shutters don't open! Mastroluca's trompe l'oeil rendering is a creative solution to the curved wall entrance of a powder room.

Design by Karyn De Boer

***Detail:* Garden Shed**
An outdoor garden shed blends with the outdoor garden
in Napa Valley, California.

***Detail:* Garden Shed**
Color and whimsy are hallmarks of this outdoor mural
by Mastroluca, who transforms an otherwise drab,
nondescript outdoor shed into a work of art.

Above:

Dining Room: Cracked Linen Walls and Border Design
Mastroluca's cracked linen technique is particularly
effective when applied over damaged walls as was the
case in this dining room. A hand-painted border, accented
with Acanthus leaves, grapes, and pomegranates, further
disguises any surface imperfections.

Left:

Powder Room: Cracked Linen Wall Panels
Mastroluca's cracked linen wall panels rendered in
coppers and golds wrap the walls and offset the
antique console table in this powder room designed
by Lila Levinson.

Photos by John Canham

Music Room

Borrowing a lacy heart-shaped design, found on embossed leather wainscoting in another part of this old Victorian mansion, and after conferring with designer Myrna Baldwin, Mastroluca paints a free-flowing frescoed design.

Photos by John Vaughan, courtesy of the artist

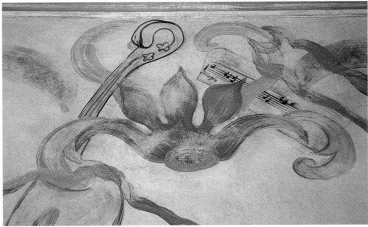

Detail: **Music Room**
Mastroluca's free-flowing border design dances about the walls of this music room.

Detail: **Music Room**
The flowing rhythms of Mastroluca's frescoed painted borders help to unify the interior of this large music room.

French Doorway

Peter Brian Daly

Peter Brian Daly holds a bachelor of science degree in fine art from the University of Bridgeport in Connecticut. He credits his university experience as well as house painting during summer vacations as ideal training for his decorative art. "I became proficient in painting in general," he says, "and in surface preparation." Much of the success of decorative art, emphasizes Daly, relies heavily on skilled preparation work.

Daly recalls a chance encounter with a decorative artist—with whom he then trained for three and a half years— as the pivotal moment influencing his career decision. He says he hasn't looked back since and opened his own studio, Artscope Enterprises in San Diego, nine years ago. Like many decorative artists, Daly continues to paint works on canvas, often rendering project proposals in the form of watercolor sketches.

Detail, French Doorway

Daly frequently translates small watercolor sketches rendered while traveling in Europe into full-scale murals, adjusting his palette to accommodate site-specific needs.

THE SIZE AND PROMINENCE OF MY CLIENT'S HOUSE AND ITS magnificent perch on the edge of a canyon factored into my decision regarding both the size and subject of this mural. As a proposal, I made a watercolor sketch recreating the California landscape—rolling hills with the canyon and hot air balloons— the very landscape one would see if the wall had windows.

The mural is large—it measures 9 feet by 13 feet (2.7 meters by 3.9 meters)—and is painted on a wall that is approximately 17 feet high (5.2 meters). To effectively translate my small watercolor rendering to such a large surface, I sketched additional pen and ink line drawings, made transparencies, and projected the final image onto the wall in two sections. I then traced the lines, adjusting compositionally as necessary. I borrowed my palette from nature. My goal was to bring the outside in, in a way that remained true to the actual sense of place. I painted in acrylics, sealing the entire surface with a satin finish.

A Gallery of Surfaces by Peter Brian Daly

Gauguin Chest

Inspired by Gauguin, Daly transforms an old lingerie chest into a piece of art furniture. Rendered in acrylics over a crackle technique, trimmed with gold, and sealed with a satin varnish, Daly's design flows asymmetrically around the piece.

My main motivation, inspiration, and desire is to master the fine art of the painted illusion. And, naturally, I want to dazzle my patron's sensibilities.

Peter Brian Daly

Daly's love of antiquity inspires many of his frescoes, which he builds using either a combination of plaster and paper pulp, or a more contemporary, lightweight foam material used by many Hollywood set designers. Daly's intent with both materials is the same—to build a fresco-like fragment patinaed with age. To do this, he primes the material and applies a crackle finish to the surface. He then overpaints the image, taking care to respect lines created by the prior cracking effect.

Living Room Mural

Daly meets the challenge to design a mural to accommodate the 9-foot by 13-foot living area (2.7-meters by 3.9-meters) in a way that works compositionally and aesthetically by painting the view to the outside of the wall.

Japanese Landscape

By thinning acrylic paints to a water-like consistency and applying to a textured wall surface, the artist achieves a mural with a painterly transparency common to the watercolor medium.

Study for a Mural
Daly's small watercolor is typical of the detailed sketches the artist renders for clients as studies for murals.

Emily's Room
Daly paints scenes from children's story books on the four walls of Emily's room. Inspired by the 9-foot (2.7-meter) ceilings, he hand brushes clouds using a reverse technique by painting blue pigment over a white ground, then wiping away the blue to reveal the clouds beneath.

The Guardian
Daly's attraction to surrealism is apparent in *The Guardian*, a study for a proposed mural, which was inspired by a dream. He describes the piece as a suggestion of old-world European but with a more modern twist.

Great Room

The artist approaches furniture design as he would a painting on canvas, rendering work in which the front relates to the back, the back to the side, and so forth. The result is a cohesive whole in which the entire environment becomes a three-dimensional work of art.

Robert A. Fischer

Calling his work "insightful," Robert Fischer applies his degree in psychology to his career as a decorative artist. He credits his ex-wife, an artist, for teaching him "the basics. She always said that it was the best thing that I didn't go to art school." Elaborating he adds, "Art schools give you absolutes. I have a natural sense for balance"—with which, he says, art school might have interfered.

Fischer calls himself a "self-taught painter with lots of taste." Critics call Fischer's boldly executed images "wittily theatrical." Saturated with color, his work is contemporary in a flashy way; his bold palette challenges. Yet Fischer manages, somehow, to compose color and design in such a way as to complement rather than compete with existing environments.

Prior to painting furniture fabrics, Fischer painted clothing. Through trial and error—and working with a paint manufacturer—he developed an acrylic paint formula to keep his fabrics looking good and feeling good. They are, he says, "durable and practical. As an artist who's working on practical objects, I have to think of these things. My furniture is very usable."

Detail, Room Divider Screen
Using gold acrylic paint on black ultra suede, the artist renders dragons on the reverse side of the screen. The paint is heavily infused with diamond dust, a pulverized glitter that adds an iridescent glow to the finished product.

I WAS ASKED TO DESIGN SOME PIECES FOR MY CLIENT'S GREAT Room. Two barrel chairs upholstered in pink silk damask caught my eye. It's wonderful to paint damask. Working with the pattern woven within the fabric, I can create great depth. It's also wonderful to take something that's old and integrate something new into the design, so I painted very contemporary portraits in contrast.

My clients then wanted a room divider screen. To integrate the screen with the chairs, I had the piece custom-made, reproducing the delicate carving of swans from the chairs in its frame which I painted metallic gold. One side of the screen is stretched with black ultra suede fabric onto which I painted gold dragons. I used a heavy acrylic gold paint infused with diamond dust, an iridescent powdered glitter that lends a wonderful sparkle and glow to the finished piece. On the other side, I stretched an ivory color imported damask fabric woven with an Art Deco circular design. To complement the barrel chairs, I painted the portraits of four very obviously dynamic women.

When all is said and done, says Fischer, "Good art is nothing more than good taste."

Room Divider Screen

Compositionally, Fischer's screen is superb. The four portraits make individual and collective statements creating a tasteful focal point in the Great Room.

Antique Barrel Chairs

The artist transforms silk damask-covered, antique barrel chairs from uninspired plain fabric into works of art. He views the challenge of merging old with new as aesthetic problem solving, saying that he believes artists must use intelligence when composing their work.

A Gallery of Surfaces by
Robert A. Fischer

I base my entire career on intuition and risk. I believe inspiration comes from everywhere. We simply need to be open to receive it—creatively and spiritually open. That's the essence of my creativity.

Robert A. Fischer

Family of Chairs
Commissioned to paint these four chairs as he wished, Fischer rendered portraits of the family in his bold and witty signature style.

***Detail,* Family of Chairs**
The artist renders each family member—and even the family horse—on the family of chairs.

***Detail,* Family of Chairs**
Customizing his work to the family's interest in tropical fish, Fischer paints one whole chair with brightly colored fish against the unifying background color palette.

"Billy Holiday" Chair

Quintessential outrageous Fischer color and pattern vibrate on the back of the round chair titled the "Billy Holiday" chair for Fischer's rendering on the front of the chair.

"Billy Holiday" Chair

Referencing an image from the Smithsonian, the artist paints a very quiet blue zebra skin on the front side of the huge round chair. Fischer varnishes all his fabrics making them practical to—in this case—curl up to sleep.

At left:

Round chairs

Fischer works with a furniture manufacturer to design these black enamel chairs with circular back panels. Inspired by an African mask, the artist layers his images to create a pattern-over-pattern effect. Then, using the same image, he alters the patterning for each chair to achieve a distinctive yet complementary effect.

Below:

Detail, **Round chairs**

"I'm all about color," says Fischer. "I don't believe there's anything like a bad color." On the reverse side of the two side chairs with the layered African mask on the front, Fischer paints two portraits of women—one an actress from the 20s sporting a big wide-brimmed hat—using intensely bright fluorescent colors.

Banquette

In the reception area of a studio for a photographer who caters to celebrities, Fischer paints furniture with famous pop images. His bold palette is in stark contrast to the all-white room.

Detail, **Banquette**

Fischer's goal in painting the recognizable faces—James Dean, Marilyn Monroe, Judy Garland, Elvis Presley—on the couch which is installed in the reception room of a photographer's studio, is to keep patrons entertained while they wait.

Pastel Chairs

Though Fischer's palette is almost exclusively bold, he describes himself as a "closet pastel person" who loves to mix exquisite pastels with casts of blues, golds, and coppers.

Pastel Chairs

Painting pastels with interference colors allows the artist to overpaint surfaces, applying, for example, blue interference over green to achieve beautiful color casts impossible with other pigment. Fischer's portraits take on an entirely different cast and depth when rendered in pastel.

Murals and Trompe l'oeil

Trompe l'oeil is the fine art of illusion, literally translated "fooling the eye." And that is precisely what artists employing trompe l'oeil techniques attempt to achieve. Their goal is to lure viewers into unquestioning acceptance that what they see, is what actually is.

Artists do not, however, achieve their intent through technical mastery alone. Creativity and imagination play a huge role, as does the need for artists to be proficient in many different genres of painting. More often than not, the successful trompe l'oeil contains paintings within the painting—landscapes and still lives for example—each of which must be rendered in proper perspective given the mural's place within the overall environment.

Trompe l'oeil fell out of favor in the late nineteenth and early twentieth century, prompted, perhaps, by a general feeling that the newly invented camera could capture the moment more successfully. Trompe l'oeil is a challenging genre. Today, artists who practice the fine art of illusion receive the credit they deserve.

Photos: (background) courtesy of Warnock Studios;
(clockwise from top) Hal Lum; Julie Sims Messenger;
courtesy of Warnock Studios; Robert Rattner; Phillip Ennis

Octagon Garden Room

After painting drifting clouds and flitting barn swallows on the 20-foot (6-meter) ceiling, the artist double-rags the garden room walls in a mossy green glaze before decorating them with lattice, wisteria, butterflies, dragon flies, bumblebees, and birds. Powers uses European stencils and trompe l'oeil painting techniques to achieve her innovative result.

Leslie Ann Powers

Decorative artist Leslie Ann Powers, retired stockbroker and statistician, works from her studio in Connecticut. Twenty years into it, she finds her career as artist satisfies her in ways Wall Street never did.

With a background in commercial art from the University of Florida, and training in the fine arts from the University of Hartford, Powers reclaims her earlier creative experiences. "My fine arts background factors in," says Powers. "Going from canvas to murals, however, is very different," she says of what she calls "two distinct disciplines." It is possible, she says, for an artist "to have marvelous skills yet not be able to translate those skills to a larger scale."

Powers also designs authentic European stencils which, unlike more simplistic American stencils, require many stencil overlaps—sometimes as many as one hundred per design. Very often, Powers combines freehand painting with European stenciling to achieve wonderfully innovative nuances in shading and detailing. So successful are stenciled effects that Powers designs stencil kits—vines, florals, animals—and markets them nationally and internationally.

***Detail,* Octagon Garden Room**
After stenciling her lattice-work pattern over walls double-ragged with a mossy green glaze, the artist adds the vines. The flexibility of her custom-designed European stencils allows her to "weave" the stenciled vines in and out of the lattice.

I STOOD IN THIS WONDERFUL OCTAGONAL ROOM WITH ITS BRICK floor, its beautiful Palladian windows and its 20-foot (6 meter) ceilings, and I said to myself, "No question, this is an English garden room," and I decided to give it a gazebo-like feeling.

Working with an assistant, I ragged several coats of medium mossy green glazes over a white background. We used several different approaches, from dragging to actually punching the rag onto the walls for a softer, more unusual look. I stenciled the lattice in a soft driftwood color, working with 20-inch (51-centimeter) stencil segments. For depth, I did a lot of overpainting, adding cracks and nail holes.

I designed sets of European stencils for the leaves, vines, and flowers and used literally hundreds of them to achieve the delicate shadings. I used, for example, fifteen different stencils for each peony, a technique that gave each flower a three-dimensional look. Then applying trompe l'oeil painting techniques, I overpainted sections. The combination—stencils and freehand—gives this mural a totally different look from a painted one.

Detail, **Cockatoo Room Divider Screen**
The artist achieves the subtle shading and detailing in her trompe l'oeil vines by overlapping layers of custom-designed European stencils.

Cockatoo Room Divider Screen
Using a combination of washes, European stenciling, overpainting, and trompe l'oeil techniques, Powers renders her design of ivy, wisteria, cockatoos, bumblebees, and dragonflies on three hollow-core door panels hinged together to make a room-divider screen.

Photos, this page by Tom Hopkins

A Gallery of Surfaces by Leslie Ann Powers

I bring my life history to my work.

My father was a scientist and a

naturalist, and I grew up camping and

hiking and mountain climbing. I'm an

avid gardener . . . . I think most of

my work is natural.

Leslie Ann Powers

***Detail,* Over Mantle Window**
Trompe l'oeil books by Powers reflect the client's hobbies and tastes.

Over Mantle Window
Inspired by an existing window in the great room of her client's home, the artist designs a trompe l'oeil window measuring 5.5 feet wide and 7 feet high (1.6 meters wide and 2.1 meters high) for the second-story landing. Powers works in acrylic on canvas, applying the finished mural directly to the wall.

Photos this page by Robert Rattner

Detail, Jacobean carpet

Working with water-based paints and polyurethane, the artist creates her Jacobean-style carpet overlapping forty custom-designed stencils to achieve a three-dimensional effect.

Photos, left and below right by Robert Rattner

Diamond Floor Pattern

After applying a background color of French blue, the artist tapes off precise diamond shapes. Using soft, cloudy off-white washes, she rags only the diamonds, finishing the entire surface with several coats of polyurethane.

Photos, below and facing page by Tom Hopkins

Jacobean carpet

Window panels in the room are the artist's inspiration for this floral design. Combining her own custom-designed European stencils with overpainting techniques, Powers lends a contemporary interpretation to the more classic Jacobean styling.

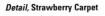

Detail, **Strawberry Carpet**
By combining overpainting with her stenciling technique, the artist adds realistic dimension to the leaves and berries.

Grapevine Border
Inspired by antique botanical paintings, the artist applies a grey-green wash to walls before applying her European stencils, which she designed in 6-foot repeats. Even with repeats, the flexibility in applying the stencils accounts for the free-flowing design.

Strawberry Carpet
The artist renders this entry carpet measuring 9 feet by 12 feet (2.7 meters by 3.7 meters) using her European stencil technique in multiple overlays to achieve subtle shadings in color and detail.

Biography Cabinet

Humor and whimsy reign in the artist's rendering of a playful "biography cabinet," of which each shelf represents the interests of individual family members. The book titles hold secret messages and tongue-in-cheek jests, while mice and rabbits scurry around making mischief. Powers' painting transforms a nondescript old cabinet into a conversation piece.

Photos, this page by Robert Rattner

Monkey Over Mantle
Solving the dilemma of what to do with a narrow mantle, Powers paints a vignette of treasured collectibles on walls first double-glazed in mossy green. The trompe l'oeil scene is playful and enhances existing themes in the house, most notably fruits, flowers, and critters.
Photo by Tom Hopkins

"Outdoor Patio"
Rendering floor tiles, stucco walls, and a trompe l'oeil vista on various thicknesses of canvas, the artist transforms a dark and uninteresting closet into an "outdoor" patio and garden planning room. She paints cabinet "windows," however, on thin board, which she then glues into place. Layers of polyurethane protect the floor canvas.
Photo by Kurt A. Dolnier / Junior League of Greenwich, CT Showhouse

"Mock" Aubusson Floorcloth

Stylized Aubusson dining room floorcloth by Julie Sims Messenger glows with
three-dimensional detailing, a hallmark of the artist's personal style. Walls
glazed by Messenger in a deep raspberry-red parchment technique complete
the dramatic ambiance of this formal room.

Photo by Kit Pyne Photography

Julie Sims Messenger

Julie Sims Messenger's background in fashion design serves her well as decorative artist. Conceptually, the two professions share similar challenges. "Fashion design trains you to consider color and texture in terms of how people live," she says. The difference is customer contact. Fashion designers create for anonymous masses whereas, says Messenger, "I interact eye-to-eye with my decorative-arts clients. I'm very fast at grasping what styles clients appreciate, or whether they respond to neutral colors or stronger, more dramatic colors. Psychological skills are important, and fashion design helped me develop these skills."

Messenger made her shift from fabric to finishes ten years ago, beginning with wall glazing which trained her to mix and conceptualize color on a large scale. Over time, she developed a personal style, narrowing her focus to custom-designed floorcloths. Messenger's translucent floorcloths glow with suggestions of eighteenth-century European opulence; they're beautiful and practical alternatives for floor coverings.

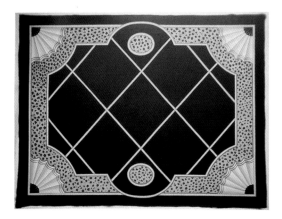

"Mock" Aubusson Floorcloth

Messenger meets the challenge of painting large floorcloths such as this "mock" Aubusson, measuring 12.5 feet by 14 feet (3.8 meters by 4.3 meters) by stapling her canvas to the wall and working from the top platform of a rolling scaffold. The translucent patterns of this black, gold, and yellow ocher floorcloth reference eighteenth-century French carpet design, imitating the look of layered carpets one on top of the other.

Photo by Julie Sims Messenger

I DESIGNED THIS MOCK AUBUSSON DINING ROOM FLOORCLOTH as a dramatic foil to the raspberry-red glazed walls, which I rendered in a basic parchment technique. It is "mock" in the sense that my design is more stylized than classic eighteenth-century French carpets. I'm inspired, however, by the color story in characteristic Aubussons—gold trompe l'oeil detailing and lots of layering to give the effect of several carpets laid one on top of the other.

I painted this 12.5-foot by 14-foot (3.8-meter by 4.3-meter) floorcloth in black with trompe l'oeil gold crisscross bars in the center, juxtaposing this with leopardskin layering to secure the dramatic effect I wanted. In each of the four corners, I painted yellow ocher quarter-fans, borrowing the design element popularized by eighteenth-century English architect Robert Adams. I used the optical illusion of the fan to effectively "frame" the drama of the floorcloth.

Detail, "Mock" Aubusson Floorcloth

In each of the four corners, trompe l'oeil gold quarter-fans, rendered in the manner of eighteenth-century English architect Robert Adam, frame the central design. To ensure balance, Messenger first tapes off part of the design, glazing or painting specific areas, section by section.

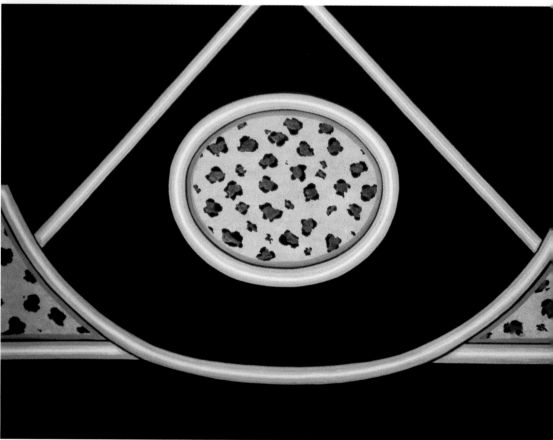

Detail, "Mock" Aubusson Floorcloth

The artist adds a contemporary flair with leopardskin detailing. To complete her work, Messenger varnishes the canvas with six coats of acrylic varnish, rolls it off the wall and finishes the edges by rolling and gluing.

Photos by Julie Sims Messenger

A Gallery of Surfaces by Julie Sims Messenger

The arts of the eighteenth century,

especially eighteenth-century France,

are a major source of inspiration for

me. I travel overseas each year to

study and absorb the extraordinary

examples of classical expression in

European architecture and design. I

love to borrow from classical styling

and make it my own.

Julie Sims Messenger

"Stone Intarsia" Dining Room Floorcloth
Messenger's "Stone Intarsia" imitates flat stone slabs, cut and fitted together in geometric patterns. This dining room floorcloth measuring 20 feet by 8.3 feet (6 meters by 2.5 meters) is precisely rendered in subtle colors—sage green and yellow ochers with red detailing.

***Detail,* "Stone Intarsia" Dining Room Floorcloth**
Details of Messenger's Stone Intarsia Dining Room Floorcloth focus on the subtle shadings and translucent glazing which are critical to the artist's successfully capturing the illusion of cut stone.

Detail, **Prussian Blue Front Hallway Floorcloth**
Messenger accomplishes a three-dimensional effect with subtle shading, all of which adds to the trompe l'oeil quality of her painted surface.

Photos, right and facing page by Julie Sims Messenger

Prussian Blue Front Hallway Floorcloth
Gold demi-fans at either end of this 9-foot by 4-foot (2.7-meter by 1.2-meter) hall carpet contain the drama of Messenger's signature design. Messenger's use of acrylic paints keeps floorcloths flexible. As long as a floorcloth is rolled up, not folded, it will last for years, says the artist.
Photo by Kit Pyne Photography

Fantasy Aubusson Floorcloth for Garden Room
Using eighteenth-century French Aubusson
carpets as her inspiration, the artist retains the
corner quarter-fan pattern, but dispenses with
classic formality of traditional Aubusson design
by introducing a more contemporary palette of
turquoises, amethysts, and soft blues.

Detail, **Fantasy Aubusson Floorcloth for Garden Room**
The traditional patterning of classical Aubussons is apparent in this corner detail with
its quarter-fan and crisscrossed gold bars layered over a turquoise ground.

Blue Monogram Floorcloth for Front Hallway

Messenger's eighteenth-century sensibilities are
apparent in this monogrammed floorcloth with its
exquisitely detailed gold design juxtaposed over its base
of rich midnight blue.

Photos by Julie Sims Messenger

Pineapple Foyer Carpet, 3.5' x 5.5' (1 m x 1.7 m)

The pineapple, the eighteenth-century's traditional symbol of "Hospitality," is the perfect choice for this foyer carpet. The artist frames her oversized botanical motif with a simple serpentine marbleized border.

***Detail*, Key Chain**

Connecting the client's personal life to the commissioned art is a frequent goal. Here, the artist paints a trompe l'oeil key chain "dropped" by front door.

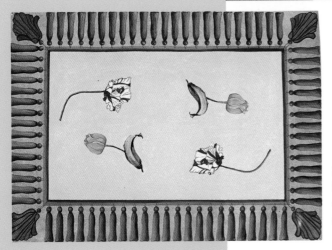

Breakfast Room Floorcloth, 4' x 6' (1.2 m x 1.8 m)

Messenger's oversized area rug features a technically superb trompe l'oeil fringe border framing a central design of scattered flowers.

Mary Jo O'Hearn

Illinois artist Mary Jo O'Hearn is relatively new to decorative arts as a business, although she worked as a professional fashion illustrator for years. In many ways, says O'Hearn, the tasks are similar. "With illustration, you learn how to make things look dimensional, and soon," she says, "the skill is second nature." The leap from fashion illustration to the painted surface is a matter of tools— exchanging pen and ink for brush and pigment. Adapting and applying her skills to trompe l'oeil painting, O'Hearn creates a nice little niche for herself—painting, among other thing, nice little niches.

Detail, Trompe l'oeil Bookshelves
Going for an uncluttered look, the artist paints books sparingly and adds accessories as decorative elements.

MY CHALLENGE WAS TO COME UP WITH AN IDEA TO SUIT A narrow landing on the fourth floor of a Chicago townhouse, a small space with just enough room for a chair and nothing more. My client was a writer and, all things considered, trompe l'oeil bookcases seemed the perfect solution. I painted a place where my client could sit to read in comfort and isolation, surrounded by "books" in a library-esque atmosphere.

I expanded the conventional idea of trompe l'oeil when I added spines of actual books to my mural, a detail that lends authenticity and interest to the finished work. My client and I decided that the bookcase should be light "oak" to match the existing banister. Reality was my goal but, unlike actual bookcases, which are often cluttered and messy, this bookcase was to be orderly and accessorized. I painted a "basket" and "plant" to hide two unsightly vents above the tall bookcase, and I "arranged" an architectural drawing, glass bowl, and fish plate as decorative displays. The client and I chose the book titles and accessories together. The whole project demonstrates my philosophy of connection.

Facing page:
Trompe l'oeil Bookshelves
Mary Jo O'Hearn's trompe l'oeil bookshelves solve the design challenge presented by a narrow fourth-floor landing in a Chicago townhouse. Viewed from below, the illusion is particularly successful.

All photos by Jinx Holesha

Detail: Trompe l'oeil Bookshelves
Painted ivy and basket successfully hide otherwise
unsightly wall vents.

Detail: Trompe l'oeil Bookshelves
Choosing book titles to reflect her client's tastes,
the artist also adds an architectural drawing as
decorative detailing.

Detail: Trompe l'oeil Bookshelves
Expanding on the concept of trompe l'oeil, O'Hearn
applies actual book bindings randomly, thus adding a
sense of authenticity and interest to her work.

A Gallery of Surfaces by Mary Jo O'Hearn

People inspire me. My challenge is to

find ways to connect—me with my

clients, and my clients with my work.

Connection is very much a part of my

creative process.

Mary Jo O'Hearn

"Carved Stone" with Chianti, African Violets, and Garlic
O'Hearn's trompe l'oeil niches are more than solutions for design challenges, they are connections. Perella is the birthplace in Italy of her client's grandparents; garlic speaks for Italian cuisine; and the stone sculpture is simply a piece of the old world.

Detail, **"Carved Stone" with Chianti, African Violets, and Garlic**
O'Hearn's painted cloth adds dimension to the small trompe l'oeil niche painted in a space too narrow and awkward to hang anything from the wall.

White Marble "Niche" with Topiary

O'Hearn's painted niches often solve design dilemmas in spaces too narrow to hang actual objects. They also offer wonderful opportunities to easily introduce color and shape. Here, the topiary and ivy inject a desired green into the palette of the room.

Detail, **White Marble "Niche" with Topiary**

In keeping with the artist's interests in connections, she paints a crystal dish to match crystal accessories gifted to her client by her mother. The "towel" is monogrammed with her client's initial and the gold ring is "just for fun as though someone had left it behind," says the artist.

Wrought Iron shelf

Drawing inspiration from a manufactured shelf, the artist reproduces it for her clients who are wine lovers.

Detail, **Wrought Iron shelf**

A loaf of challa sits on the faux bois shelf, which is held up by the trompe l'oeil wrought iron frame in O'Hearn's painted niche.

Gray Stone Shelf

Painted in the kitchen over the table, the composition of this trompe l'oeil with its wine bottle, cherub statuary, topiary ivy, and linen cloth adds color and dimension to what was a blank and uninteresting wall.

Cherry Shelf with Blue and White Plate
O'Hearn personalizes her trompe l'oeil shelf with pottery patterns lifted from fabric designs in the nearby kitchen.

Oak Shelf with Chianti and Grapes
Ever mindful of shape and form, O'Hearn chooses grapes to introduce color, and cloth for shape and dimension in this kitchen "shelf." To contrast with detailed architectural paintings rendered elsewhere in the room, the artist opted for simplicity.

Arched Niche

Two books, gold earrings, wine glass, and monogrammed napkin "belong" to the clients for whom the artist rendered this arched niche in the master bedroom of a Chicago loft.

Detail, Arched Niche

Inspired by a photograph of a charming European doorway and window, the artist adds the patina of age apparent in the worn and wonderful book jackets.

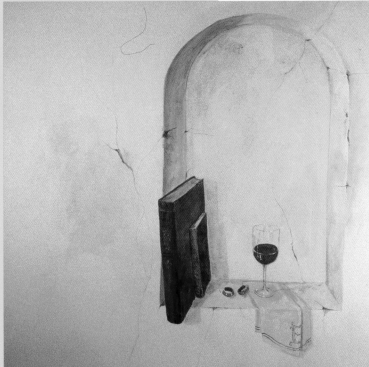

Ocher Colored Marble Corner Shelf

O'Hearn's painted illusion connects master bath "spa" to master bedroom. Accessorized with plants, candles and bottles of oil—items appropriate to a spa—the end result is decidedly European in flavor.

Exercise Room

Working with a bold color palette and a fluid design concept, the artist transforms an oddly shaped exercise room into a stimulating environment.

Patti Bruce

Patti Bruce shies away from labels. "I hate to be categorized as having a certain style," says the self-taught decorative artist whose Hawaii-based business is over a decade old. Bruce speaks with the authority of years of experience and a portfolio that supports her claim to diversity.

She does, however, demonstrate a quality and essence of style that is uniquely her own. There is a graphic element to much of her work, illustrating the ease with which she uses form and colors to compose her decorative arts commissions. Her projects are collaborations between her clients and her own artistic sensibilities. At times, Bruce's work is abstract; at other times her more precise interpretations stand in dramatic contrast to her more loosely stylized work.

***Detail*, Exercise Room**

Viewing the simple silhouettes as negative and positive shape, Bruce planned her layout carefully, mindful of the effects of overlapping pigment.

DEVELOPING AN APPROPRIATE DESIGN CONCEPT FOR AN exercise room isn't easy. With its five walls, this oddly shaped room was particularly difficult. A rerun of the old Alfred Hitchcock movie, beginning with Hitchcock's silhouette, triggered my idea to paint silhouettes of figures engaged in a variety of athletic activities. With the theme set, I established the scene, which was inspired by Ala Moana Beach Park where people jog and watch the sunset.

I didn't want floating silhouettes, so I established a horizon line, air brushed clouds on the ceiling, sponged ground about a third of the way up the wall, and created a stylized park at sunset. Dealing with negative and positive space was the challenge, and how overlapping pigment would interact within each space. To help me solve these problems, I projected stylized figures onto the wall, juxtaposed them, overlapped them, worked on perspective, and planned my layout. I also developed my palette. I used acrylics and a water-based sealer. The end result, I think, is a stimulating and colorful environment where the visuals make the room an exciting place to be.

Detail, Exercise Room

This exercise room presents nooks
and crannies and oddly shaped areas
which Bruce approaches as
individual "murals" within the
context of the whole.

A Gallery of Surfaces by Patti Bruce

I take my inspiration from the

environment in which I'm working. I'm

really trying to capture the entire

essence of a room, something that fits

in the client's home with the client's

lifestyle, and I use color, form, and

shape in ways that fit.

Patti Bruce

With a little paint and a lot of imagination, Bruce creates joyful children's furniture.

At left:
ABC Furniture

Below right:
Birthday Furniture

Below left:
Fish Furniture

Master Bathroom, Bamboo

To soften the whiteness of the bathroom walls, Bruce applies a mauve glaze, which she fades from floor to ceiling. In keeping with the Asian theme of the home decor, she paints swaying elephant bamboo fronds.

Detail, **Master Bathroom, Bamboo**

By wrapping the bamboo fronds up and around the corner, the artist achieves a free-flowing, natural effect.

Cupid Niche
Adding interest as a backdrop to the client's prized sculpture of Cupid, Bruce paints a niche at the entrance to a dining room.

Powder Room
A simple arch divides a tiny powder room—water closet on one side, vanity on the other. Bruce works with the existing architecture to render two scenes, the first indoor. But walk through the archway and you are "outside," overlooking the bay and ruins in the distance.

Dining Room, Moroccan Tent

The styling of the "tented" fabric walls in their soft colors offers
tranquility. Smith's market scene adds color and motion to what might
otherwise become a static space.

James Alan Smith

James Alan Smith holds a masters degree in Dance from Ohio State University. It is dance that lured him to New York over sixteen years ago; it is art that compels him to stay. Smith credits his mentor, the late Richard Lowell Neaps, with helping him to break into the fine art of the decorative arts. "I ended up assisting him as well as doing lots of jobs for him," says Smith. "It was very much the old Guild system; I learned from the master."

Smith also credits his schooling at the Isabelle O'Neill Foundation in New York, first as student and later as teacher, as furthering his individual style and aiding his professional development.

Today, the artist works from his studio in Water Mill, Long Island. His often lyrical style references his familiarity and comfort with the physicality of movement, which he sees as integral to any successfully composed work of art. Of his work he says, "I'm almost physically involved, the synapses from my brain to my hands are one."

Photos by Phillip Ennis

Detail, Dining Room, Moroccan Tent
Pattern-on-pattern is very Moroccan, and the artist plays with this design hallmark as he overlays painted swags and borders with planned abandon.

INTERESTINGLY, MY CLIENTS ORIGINALLY WANTED A KIND OF "Out of Africa" mural with trees, lions, and giraffes. As fate would have it, they happened to see an image in Vogue that caught their imagination; it was the background scene of a fashion shoot with a Moroccan flavor. I ripped up my preliminary sketch and submerged myself in research. The dining room is large. I felt a Moroccan tent-like wall and ceiling treatment would create consistency, yet allow me to paint interest and motion in select areas.

To accomplish a compositionally effective tenting of the wall "fabric," I first rendered a charcoal drawing; when translating the drawing to the wall surface, I adjusted elements for scale where necessary. I then painted in all the shadows. Next, using shades of umber and gray, I painted the folds in the fabric. The striping came last, rendered in shades of muted terra cotta colors beginning with the lightest color. In areas where the stripes met the fold, I added additional shading. The illusion complete, I was free to focus on individual wall surfaces, treating each as mini-murals within the larger mural.

Detail, Dining Room, Moroccan Tent

At the client's suggestion, a tiger lounges outside the "tent," an unthreatening member of the scene thanks to extensive research on Smith's part. "I didn't want him to be foreboding in any way; I wanted him to be soothing," he says.

Photos by Phillip Ennis

The artist creates an intimate eating area in a "tented" corner of the room. The trompe l'oeil grate adds an asymmetrical touch, one of the backbones of Smith's design philosophies.

A Gallery of Surfaces by James Alan Smith

My belief is that all art forms are the

same . . . . whether you have a phrase

of music or a design concept, you can

manipulate it by inverting it, retrograding

it, augmenting it, diminishing it. You can

do that with your body, and you can do

it with design. In my art, I'm very

influenced by dance and movement.

James Alan Smith

Trompe l'oeil Window
In a renovated beach house, Smith paints the scene a viewer would see if, in fact, a window existed instead of the wall. He uses oil-based flat paint with no finish, rendering the scene in a style more photographic than stylistic.

Trompe l'oeil Refrigerator Door Panel
One of the features of the Subzero refrigerator is a door panel, which can be changed at will. At the client's request, Smith paints a trompe l'oeil on a 1/8"-thick piece of wood which he then inserts into the refrigerator door panel. Everything from the Nantucket baskets to the dinner plates and folk-art slice of watermelon have meaning for the client.

Photos courtesy of the artist

Trompe l'oeil Door

Smith solves a design challenge in an apartment with more than its share of hallways and doors by disguising a door inconveniently located in the middle of his mural. Adding architectural elements and Corinthian pilasters rendered on a faux limestone wall, the artist successfully creates his illusion.

***Detail,* Trompe l'oeil Door**

Influenced by Dutch Master paintings, and as a tribute to his own mother, Smith paints a vase of flowers into the trompe l'oeil niche of his disguised door.

Photos, this page courtesy of the artist

Child's Bedroom

In keeping with the contemporary ambiance of a city apartment, Smith's colorful mural tumbles across the walls of this child's bedroom. The mural is rendered on canvas and applied to the walls to facilitate removal should the client move or when the child outgrows its playful theme.

Photos, this page by Phillip Ennis

***Detail,* Entryway**

The artist accentuated existing architectural detailing including the ribbing of the vaulted ceiling where he added faux brick reminiscent of Medieval France.

Photos by Phillip Ennis

At left:

Entryway

Smith adds charm and illusion to a small townhouse entryway separated from the street with wrought iron gates. Faux limestone-blocked walls frame the artist's painted French chateau to one side, and a vase of flowers inspired by Dutch Masters, to the other.

Facing page:

Parquet Floor

It is Smith's parquet-patterned painted floor that adds the detail and whimsy to this intimate dining area off the living room. In developing his "parquet" pattern, he gives area dimensions and design to an architect to computer-generate a grid from which Smith works. He tapes out his patterns, hand paints with Japan oils, and seals with a polyurethane.

Library Ceiling

Drawing inspiration from historical maps rendered in the 1600s, the artists begin by brushing prepared canvas with glazes to replicate old tea-stained paper. Painted in the studio in two pieces sliced at the equator, the map requires the hands of several people to install.

Warnock Studios

After a decade of mastering the basics, the Warnocks feel free to experiment. "The availability of new materials allows us to do many decorative techniques differently from our predecessors, more easily and more dramatically," says Liz, who, with her husband Tom, operates Warnock Studios in Washington, D.C. The company employs eight formally trained artists who, says Tom, "add depth and inspiration to each project."

Liz holds an MFA from the University of Alabama, although prior to launching Warnock Studios over a decade ago, she belonged to corporate America. Tom's background is in broadcasting— photography and video—and he credits years of training his eye to visually compose his subjects as invaluable in his current profession.

Historic influences are evident in Liz and Tom's carefully researched work, which is visually and emotionally compelling.

Detail, Library Ceiling
To break vast areas of uncharted space, the artists pull decorative elements such as this sea monster from various historic maps.

OUR POINT OF DEPARTURE WAS A MATTER-OF-FACT DIRECTIVE to paint an old world map on the ceiling of the library in the client's home. Research engaged the two of us throughout step one. We came up with a variety of historical examples of maps; we provided copies to the clients, studied their reactions— what they liked and disliked—and developed a hybrid blend of varying elements. Since most old-world maps have vast areas of uncharted territory, we used artistic license to enlarge entire continents and fill voids to satisfy our aesthetic.

Working on canvas in our studio, we began by slicing the map on the equator to facilitate installation and eliminate distracting joins. We rendered the border design in one long strip, mitering the corners and applying it separately.

Our painterly charge was to make the map look old and stained, as if it had been rolled and unrolled many times. We began by brushing the canvas with a wall glaze, giving the effect of old tea-stained paper. Using portrait oils and a very narrow palette that included all the earth tones—umbers, siennas, ochers—we tried to paint the effect of watercolor, torturing the surface with sprays of mineral spirits, and rubbing back with cheesecloth to achieve the patina of age.

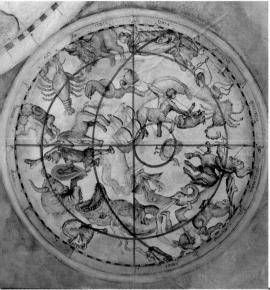

Detail, Library Ceiling

Approaching the decorative border of the ceiling mural much like wallpaper borders, the artists render their design on one long strip of canvas which they then apply separately, taking care to miter each corner.

Detail, Library Ceiling

Adding elements such as this celestial chart with its pictorial representations of the Zodiac, the artists meet the challenge of aesthetically composing the mural, which measures 15.5 feet by 22 feet (4.7 meters by 6.7 meters) and will be viewed from below.

Detail, Library Ceiling

Using astrological devices as decorative elements, the artists anchor the two globes to create a cohesive overall ceiling pattern.

A Gallery of Surfaces by
Warnock Studios

The colors of nature inspire us . . . .

shadows at various times of the day . . . .

a mindfulness of what we see inspires

us all the time. And while most our

work comes from the past, we're more

and more open to incorporating the

spirit of the old masters with cutting-

edge contemporary, giving us some

pretty exciting mixes.

Liz and Tom Warnock

Above:

Foyer

Rendering a limestone finish on drywall, the artists use a grisaille technique working in varying shades of one color, in this case neutral earth tones. To achieve the effect of limestone, the artists pad the surface with unprinted newsprint.

At Left:

***Detail*, Foyer**

To the right and left of the arched doorway and above the chair rail, the artists pull the composition together with a painted border of bound laurel, and a pattern known as Prince of Wales.

Above:

Meditation Room

Silence reigns in this carefully composed meditation room with its decidedly Moroccan ambiance. To achieve the tiled floor effect, the artists first applied gold leaf to tempered Masonite cut to fit the site. A midnight blue stencil pattern suggestive of ceramic tile is sealed with a high-tech water-based catalytic polymer.

At left:

Detail, **Meditation Room**

The artists apply tinted varnishes to their surface design patterns, creating additional interest and shadowing.

Detail, **Meditation Room**

Using pattern-on-pattern, the artists glaze and stencil the walls. They achieve an old worn effect by attacking the surface with kitchen scrubbies, wearing back layers of color to reveal the layers beneath.

Library mural

The Warnocks are not without humor, and often add quirky contemporary elements to their work, such as the rider with sunglasses, another wearing a watch.

Detail, **Library Mural**

Referencing a painting seen in Florence in one of the Medici palaces, the artists recreate the Journey of the Magi on their client's library wall. The mural is rendered in oil on canvas in the artists' studio, then applied to the curved wall beneath the stairs.

Breakfast Room

Working in their studio, the artists transform sheets of 4 foot by 8 foot (1.2 meters by 2.4 meters) tempered Masonite into the illusion of an old ceramic tiled floor. Overglazing a background field of yellow with burnt sienna, the artists then mask off and glaze each tile separately to achieve a natural break in the color patterning.

Detail, Breakfast Room

Stenciling their design over layers of burnt sienna glazes, the artists seal the surface with an oil-base varnish simulating the look of ceramic tile. They hand paint the grout lines last.

Facing page:

Oriental Mural

Meeting the challenge presented by the curved passageway on the upper level of their clients' home, the artists borrow images from antique Oriental screens to render an 8-foot by 20-foot (2.4 m x 6 m) mural. Covering the surface with composition gold leaf ground, the artists manipulate robin's egg blue glaze with cheesecloth to create an amorphous "fog" of softened color beneath the gilded clouds.

Heraldic ceiling

Each individual heraldic design is 3 feet by 3 feet (.91 meters by .91 meters), painted on canvas prepared to resemble the texture of old leather. The artists then apply gilt to the entire surface, over which they paint all the decorative elements. From the floor, viewers catch a glint of the gold leafing beneath the painted surface designs.

Directory

Decorative Artists

Bopas, Inc.
Robert Grady
Gedes Paskauskas
30 Ipswich Street
Boston, MA 02215
Tel: (617) 236-4919
Fax: (617) 266-0725
page 4, 11, 12–19

Patti Bruce Decorative Art
4614 Kilanea Avenue, Suite 312
Honolulu, HI 96816
Tel/Fax: (808) 926-8866
page 107, 132–137

Charlene "Charley" Ayuso Cooper
FAUXFinish Studio, Inc.
700 Evans Creek Court
San Ramon, CA 94583
Tel: (925) 551-7732
Fax: (925) 833-0373
e-mail: FAUXCEO@aol.com
page 11, 20–27

Peter Brian Daly
Artscope Enterprizes
2961 Columbia Street #16
San Diego, CA 92103
Tel: (619) 230-9138
page 92–97

Helen R. Doane
653 Main Street
Harwich, MA 02645
Tel: (508) 432-5548
page 53, 54–61

Jeff Entner
577A State Road
Vineyard Haven, MA 02568
Tel: (508) 693-5845
page 11, 28–35

Joe Fenzl
Decorative Arts of Los Angeles
1618 1/2 Euclid Street
Santa Monica, CA 90404
Tel/Fax: (310) 396-8636
page 11, 36–43

Robert A. Fischer
Palm Springs, CA 92264
Represented by Patrick Sheehan
(See Additional Resources listing)
page 98–105

Robert Grady
Bopas, Inc.
30 Ipswich Street
Boston, MA 02215
Tel: (617) 236-4919
Fax: (617) 266-0725
page 4, 12–19

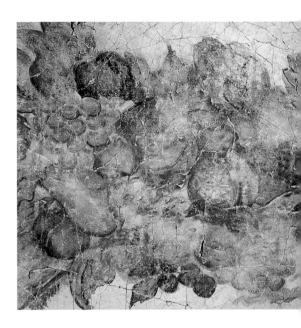

Martin Alan Hirsch
Decorative Finishes Studio
1905 Bardstown Road
Louisville, KY 40205
Tel: (800) 598-FAUX (-3289)
Fax: (502) 473-1562
www.fauxfinish.com
page 11, 44–51

Suzanne Mastroluca
Impressions In Paint
1509 Alma Terrace
San Jose, CA 95125
Tel: (408) 286-4460
Fax: (408) 286-4112
page 53, 84–91

Kathy McDonald, Designer
5 N. 411 Harvest Lane
St. Charles, IL 60175
Tel/Fax: (630) 377-5167
page 53, 62–69

Julie Sims Messenger
Art Floorcloths
Tel: (781) 545-6569
page 107, 116–123

Michael Tyson Murphy
135 West 20th Street #400
New York, NY 10011
Tel: (212) 989-0180
Fax: (212) 989-0443
page 78–83

Mary Jo Parker O'Hearn
1636 77th Court
Elmwood Park, IL 60707
Tel: (708) 456-4065
page 107, 124–131

John Parsons
7 Seymour Street
Quincy, MA 02169
Tel: (617) 328-0155
page 53, 70–77

Gedes Paskauskas
Bopas, Inc.
30 Ipswich Street
Boston, MA 02215
Tel: (617) 236-4919
Fax: (617) 266-0725
page 4, 12–19

Leslie Ann Powers
European Stenciling, Trompe l'oeil & Murals
241 State Street
Guilford, CT 06437
Tel/Fax: (203) 453-9583
page 108–115

James Alan Smith
Decorative Hand Painting
83 Halsey Lane
Water Mill, NY 11976
Tel: (516) 726-5401
page 107, 138–145

Additional Resources

Isaac Bailey Photography
P.O. Box 954
San Ramon, CA 94583
Tel: (925) 828-6555
e-mail: isaac@ifn.net
www.ifn.net/users/isaac
page 11, 20, 21

Myrna L. Baldwin
Baldwin Interiors
20465 Saratoga-Los Gatos Road
Saratoga, CA 95070
Tel: (408) 741-5003

Beacon Hill Showroom
1 Design Center Place
Suite 200
Boston, MA 02210
Tel: (617) 482-6600

James A. Brown Photography
11684 Ventura Boulevard, Suite 615
Studio City, CA 91604
page 98–105

John Canham
Quadra Focus Photography
588 Waite Avenue
Sunnyvale, CA 94086
Tel: (408) 739-1465
Fax: (408) 739-9117
page 90

Chris Covey
Photographer
Tel: (310) 373-4073
page 11, 42

Karyn DeBoer
Tollgate Interiors
14414 Oak Street
Saratoga, CA 95070
Tel: (408) 741-5177
page 89

Dale Michaels Wade
625 Bridge Road
Eastham, MA 02642
Tel: (508) 255-1371
Fax: (508) 255-6328
page 53, 54–61

Warnock Studios
Fine Surface Decoration
Thomas Warnock
Elizabeth Warnock
3245 Nebraska Avenue N.W.
Washington, DC 20016
Tel/Fax: (202) 537-0134
page 107, 146–153

Kurt A. Dolnier
c/o Leslie Ann Powers
(See Additional Resources listing)
page 115

Phillip H. Ennis
98 Smith Street
Freeport, NY 11520
Tel: (516) 379-4273
page 106–107, 138–140, 143–145

Dan Fenzl
fatalist@mediaone.net
page 36, 37, 38, 39, 40, 41

Fox-Nahem Design
69 Fifth Avenue
New York, NY 10003
Tel: (212) 929-1485
Fax: (212) 645-3136

R. FitzGerald & Company, Inc.
Interior Design
575 Boylston Street
Boston, MA 02116-3607
Tel: (617) 266-6500
Fax: (617) 266-5288

Irene Genung
Calligraphy
Tel: (510) 481-8191

James M. Goodnough Photography
38 Whiffletree Avenue
Brewster, MA 02631
Tel: (508) 385-7229
page 9, 53, 54, 57, 58, 59, 60, 61

Sam Gray Photography
23 Westwood Road
Wellesley, MA 02181
Tel: (617) 237-2711

Jinx Holesha
1626 75th Avenue
Elmwood Park, IL 60707
Tel: (708) 456-0974
page 124–131

Tom Hopkins
2121 Durham Road
Madison, CT 06443
Tel: (203) 421-4644
Fax: (203) 421-5582
page 108–110, 112, 113, 115

Peter Jaquith Photography
6 Pleasant Street
Beverly, MA 01915
Tel: (978) 921-4737

Ellen Lemer Korney
10170 Culver Boulevard
Culver City, CA 90232
Tel: (310) 204-6576
page 9, 11, 41, 42

Dennis Krukowski
Fine Interior Photography
329 East 92 Street, Suite 1D
New York, NY 10128
Tel: (212) 860-0912
Fax: (212) 860-0913
page 78–83

Pat Larin, ASID
12720 Dianne Drive
Los Altos, CA 94022
Tel: (415) 941-4611

Lila Levinson, ASID, CKD, CID
2075 DeLa Cruz Blvd., #101
Santa Clara, CA 95050
Tel: (408) 988-4600

Hal Lum
1717 Citron Street #703
Honolulu, HI 96826
Tel: (808) 941-6241
page 106, 132–137

Sauson Luongo
52 Dela Park road
Westwood, MA 02098
page 31, 32, 34

Bruce T. Martin Photography
17 Tudor Street
Cambridge, MA 02139
Tel: (617) 492-8009
Fax: (617) 492-4503
page 13, 14, 19

Randy McCaffery Photography
Tel: (502) 584-2774
www.aye.net/~mccaffry
page 11, 43–51

Daniel McManus Photography
15 Thurston Avenue
Newport, RI 02840
Tel: (401) 849-8652
page 11, 15, 16, 18

Malgosia Migdal
468 North Camden Drive, Suite 200
Beverly Hills, CA 90210
Tel: (310) 285-5366

Susan Neddich
c/o Bopas
(See Additional Resources listing)

Kit Pyne Photography
8 Union Park Street
Boston, MA 02118
Tel: (617) 542-4898
page 116, 120

Robert Rattner
P.O. Box 3362
Stony Creek, CT 06405
Tel: (203) 488-2031
Fax: (203) 488-6071
page 106–107, 111, 112, 114

Reddick Design
1950 Massachusetts Avenue
Cambridge, MA 02140
Tel: (617) 868-7336
Fax: (617) 868-3182

Kelli Ruggere Photography
423 West Broadway
South Boston, MA 02127
Tel: (617) 269-4683
Fax: (617) 335-5225
page 53, 70–77

Patrick Sheehan
Artist's Representative
1257 Granvia Valmonte
Palm Springs, CA 92262
Tel: (760) 325-1932

Peter Simon Photography
Chilmark, MA
Tel: (508) 645-9575
page 11, 28, 29, 30, 33, 34, 35

Jim Stob
42 W 704 Bridle Court
St. Charles, IL 60175
Tel: (630) 584-4120
Fax: (630) 377-3961
page 53, 62–69

Sandra J. Tuthill, ASID
Interior Design
7 Eagle Drive
Mashpee, MA 02649
Tel: (508) 539-1665
Fax: (508) 477-6835
page 74

Vince Valdes Photography
10 Liberty Ship Way #250
Sausalito, CA 94965
Tel: (415) 381-2811
Fax: (415) 383-8974
page 53, 84

John Vaughan
c/o Suzanne Mastrolvca
(See Additional Resources listing)
page 86, 87, 88, 89, 91

Sin ser faro ni roca
I AM NOT A LIGHTHOUSE OR A ROCK.
En medio del mar estoy,
BUT I LIVE AT THE END OF THE SEA.
También estoy en la playa:
YOU'LL ALSO FIND ME IN THE SAND:
¡Adivinen, pues, quién soy!
NOW GUESS WHO I MIGHT BE.

Un Caracol ~ a Seashell

Vineyard Decorators
835 Airport Road
Vineyard Haven, MA 02568
Tel: (508) 693-9197

Marjorie Wallace Interior design
2426 Pomino Way
Pleasanton, CA 94566
Tel: (925) 846-1978
page 22, 23, 24, 25, 26, 27

About the Author

Karen Aude is an arts writer and collage artist. Her articles have been published in several regional and national magazines and newspapers, and she is the author of *Heather Braginton-Smith,* a monograph on the work of the trompe l'oeil artist. Aude lives in Yarmouth Port, Massachusetts with her two feline companions, Bohditree and Sami.